The Complete OCD Workbook

THE COMPLETE OCD WORKBOOK

A STEP-BY-STEP GUIDE TO FREE YOURSELF FROM INTRUSIVE THOUGHTS AND COMPULSIVE BEHAVIORS

SCOTT GRANET, LCSW

ALTHEA
PRESS

For general information on our other products and services or to obtain technical support, please contact our Customer Care Department within the United States at (866) 744-2665, or outside the United States at (510) 253-0500.

Althea Press publishes its books in a variety of electronic and print formats. Some content that appears in print may not be available in electronic books, and vice versa.

Interior Designer: Katy Brown
Cover Designer: Kristine Brogno
Editor: Nana K. Twumasi
Production Editor: Andrew Yackira

ISBN: Print 978-1-64152-017-1 | eBook 978-1-64152-018-8

CONTENTS

INTRODUCTION

I MAJORED IN PSYCHOLOGY in college and later went on to get a master's degree in social work. I knew that I eventually wanted a career in psychotherapy, but beyond that I didn't really have an idea of any particular specialty. That changed in 1982, when I was employed as a social worker for a large nursing home in San Francisco. It was my job to tend to the psychosocial needs of the residents, which required getting to know several hundred people. On one occasion, I was asked to visit a 91-year-old woman who hadn't let anyone into her room for several months, with the exception of infrequent visits from nurses and her doctor. The social worker before me had worked there for several years and had seen her only a few times. Now it was my turn.

The first time I knocked on her door, she didn't respond. This was true for many a time after that. I don't recall how many times I walked away without meeting her, but one day the door opened. I'd been told that she was diagnosed with obsessive-compulsive disorder (OCD), and although I had some idea what that meant, I was unprepared for what I saw. She, and everything in her room, was covered either with cloth or paper towels. In fact, she opened her door while holding a tissue and asked that I sit down in a chair that was covered with towels. Her entire apartment and everything in it—pillows, blankets, bookshelf, window ledge, television, radio—and her body were all covered in towels.

We actually got along quite well. I would visit her most weeks, and she would tell me various stories about her life. It wasn't my role to do any psychotherapy with her, and I'm doubtful she would have allowed that anyway. I don't think we really even discussed her OCD much, with the exception of her telling me that she was protecting herself from germs. She warned me to be more careful when it came to touching items around the facility because the place was fraught with all sorts of dangers. In her mind, living in a nursing home meant no shortage of life-threatening situations she could encounter.

This was my first exposure to someone with OCD. I was so fascinated with her stories and behavior that I used her as my case to present to the California Board of Behavioral Sciences for my licensing exam. I learned all I could about OCD and later became a member of the International OCD Foundation (IOCDF), which at the time was called the Obsessive-Compulsive Foundation. Shortly thereafter I became a founding member of the board of directors for OCD San Francisco, an affiliate organization of the IOCDF. As my specialty in OCD grew, I learned that I liked to teach and began offering workshops throughout the country on both OCD and body dysmorphic disorder (BDD). I've taught at many continuing education programs throughout the country, including those that are university-based and those offered by private companies. I've given numerous presentations at the IOCDF annual conferences and developed an anxiety disorders certificate program for the University of California at Berkeley Extension. To date, I have probably trained several thousand therapists in the treatment of OCD, BDD, and anxiety disorders.

For 27 years, I worked at Palo Alto Medical Foundation Department of Psychiatry and Behavioral Health. It was there that I truly developed my specialty. For about 20 of those years, I ran an OCD treatment group in addition to seeing patients individually. During much of that time I also participated in my private practice. In 2008 I opened the OCD-BDD Clinic of Northern California. Today I work exclusively in my practice, where approximately 90 percent of my patients have either OCD or BDD.

When I first considered writing a book on OCD, I wondered what expertise I could offer that doesn't already exist in other books. I thought that perhaps a book that focuses almost exclusively on treatment was the right way to go. I knew that I still needed to offer the basics of describing OCD, but I didn't want to spend too much time on that, since this book is really written for people with OCD themselves—the individuals who know more about it than anyone. In this book I focus more on how to get to the problems associated with the disorder as quickly as possible. What you'll find here is an introductory chapter on the disorder, then a deep exploration into treatment. Much of the book concentrates on exposure and response prevention (ERP) therapy, the gold standard for treating OCD. Along the way we will also explore other forms of treatment that over the years have become part of the tool kit in treating OCD. This includes cognitive therapy, acceptance and commitment therapy (ACT), and the meditative practice of mindfulness.

Given that this is a workbook, you will be put to work. There are opportunities throughout for you to address your own obsessions and compulsions. Together we will look at building an effective, long-lasting plan to help you learn how to gain better control over your OCD.

One final note before we get to chapter 1: You're not in this alone. As I tell my patients, treating OCD is meant to be a collaborative effort—you and me working as a team to overcome the disorder. I know that you're going to be doing most of the work, but you'll have my guidance along the way. I want you to know that we're in this together.

A DISCLAIMER

AS YOU WILL NOTICE THROUGHOUT THIS BOOK, OCD comes in many, many forms. You likely already know about several of them, but some are possibly going to be new to you. Some may seem to be quite silly while others may seem downright scary. In the latter category are the obsessions associated with harming oneself or harming others as well as those pertaining to intrusive thoughts of sexual content, such as child molestation. It's all OCD. Most people will agree that the more commonly recognized forms of OCD, such as compulsive handwashing and the checking of doors, make little sense. The same is true for the more disturbing obsessions you are going to encounter in this book. They, too, make little sense.

I react to all forms of OCD in the same manner: The obsessions and compulsions have nothing to do with someone's character. They merely are manifestations of the disorder. I do recognize, however, that the harm and sexual obsessions are often the most troubling. Even so, they are still just symptoms of OCD and are not any more significant than any others. So, if you are shocked by some of what you read, please put it in the proper context of it all being part of the same problem.

Exposure and response prevention therapy will be thoroughly explored in this book, as it is the treatment of choice for OCD. It is important that readers understand that exposing themselves to fearful thoughts is a necessary part of the process. Our goal is to get you to the point where these troubling thoughts lose their hold over you. No one can ever promise you that these thoughts will go away entirely, so instead our focus needs to be on learning to live with them and getting you to the point where you are more in control of them than they are of you.

I often recommend books to my clients, but sometimes people tell me that they are afraid to read them because they don't want to read about people who are also struggling with OCD and about their troubling obsessions and compulsions. While this workbook is meant as a guide to assist you in learning the tools needed to better cope with the disorder, some of what you read may trigger uncomfortable feelings for you. That is normal and to be expected. Read the book at a pace that feels manageable to you, but read the book completely. If you find yourself triggered as you read, take that as an opportunity to do more exposure therapy. If you experience the temptation to skip over sections you find to be especially troubling, it's a sign that those are the parts to which you need to pay particular attention. Avoidance is a primary coping strategy for many people with OCD. It's also a very ineffective one, as I'm sure you have found. Please stick to the reading and do the suggested exercises. If you do so, I'm confident that you will find it to be an enlightening and ultimately rewarding experience.

PART ONE

UNPACKING OCD & EXPLORING TREATMENT

CHAPTER ONE

Over and Over Again

LIVING WITH OCD CAN BE VERY HARD; so is the process of learning the skills that you need in order to cope with it. I'm hopeful, however, that you will find the progression ultimately very gratifying. So, congratulations on taking this first step toward confronting your disorder. As you embark on the journey of gaining better control over your OCD, this first chapter will explain what the term actually means, from both a day-to-day perspective and a clinical one. These days, it's common to hear the phrase "I'm so OCD" jokingly tossed around. It's highly unlikely that people saying that really understand what the disorder is all about. This chapter will look at what it means to truly have OCD and the many ways it can manifest itself. We'll start with a story of someone who has lived with OCD, then take a look at possible causes of it, followed by an overview of how I believe this book can be of help.

I Keep Getting Stuck

Kevin is a 14-year-old high school freshman who first began showing signs of OCD when he was in sixth grade. When completing homework assignments, Kevin often felt the need to erase his work if one letter touched another. Unlike many people with OCD, Kevin wasn't worried that anything bad would happen to him or anyone else if he didn't perform this task. Rather, he was overcome by the feeling that he had to complete his work in a certain way until it felt right.

At that point, no one who knew Kevin saw this behavior as OCD related but rather as an unusual quirk. But it did create problems for him on tests. Kevin would typically run out of time to complete them. He usually knew the answers, but he just couldn't finish the work fast enough. Even though Kevin didn't complete many tests and assignments, he managed to get through middle school and was promoted to high school.

This manifestation of the OCD seemed to subside some over the summer months, but when Kevin returned to school in the fall as a freshman, everything shifted. Now the OCD started to exhibit through other behaviors that involved walking, closing doors, and turning off lights. Again, he wasn't worried about anything bad happening to him or anyone else if he didn't complete these tasks—a common thought among many people with OCD. Instead, Kevin felt compelled to behave in a certain manner until the anxiety went away. Once the behavior was completed, that was when he would achieve that "just right" feeling.

Walking became particularly problematic. Whenever Kevin saw a line or a crack in the pavement, he had to step back and forth over it three times while also turning his head to the right. This was very different from his previous OCD behavior. With homework, it wasn't evident that Kevin was doing anything unusual, but now his behavior was more obvious. This led Kevin to feel embarrassed and ashamed of his actions. The behavior didn't happen just at school. It happened at home, while hanging out with friends, and when in public.

When Kevin's parents began to notice an increase in these behaviors, they took him to his pediatrician, who suggested that he might have OCD. He was then referred to me. When Kevin told me about his symptoms, I knew right away that he was experiencing "just right" OCD. I explained to him and his parents that this common form of OCD essentially describes people who have to complete an action (and/or thought) until they feel "just right." While many people with OCD may worry about bad things happening to themselves or loved ones under similar circumstances, Kevin instead experienced an uncomfortable feeling that wouldn't go away unless he completed the required compulsion. As is often the case for many people and families living with OCD, Kevin and his parents were relieved to know that there was a name for his problem. They were also thrilled to learn that there is effective treatment for it. At the same time, they were also understandably frightened over what it might mean for his future.

How about you? What's your reaction to Kevin's story? Does it resonate with you in some way?

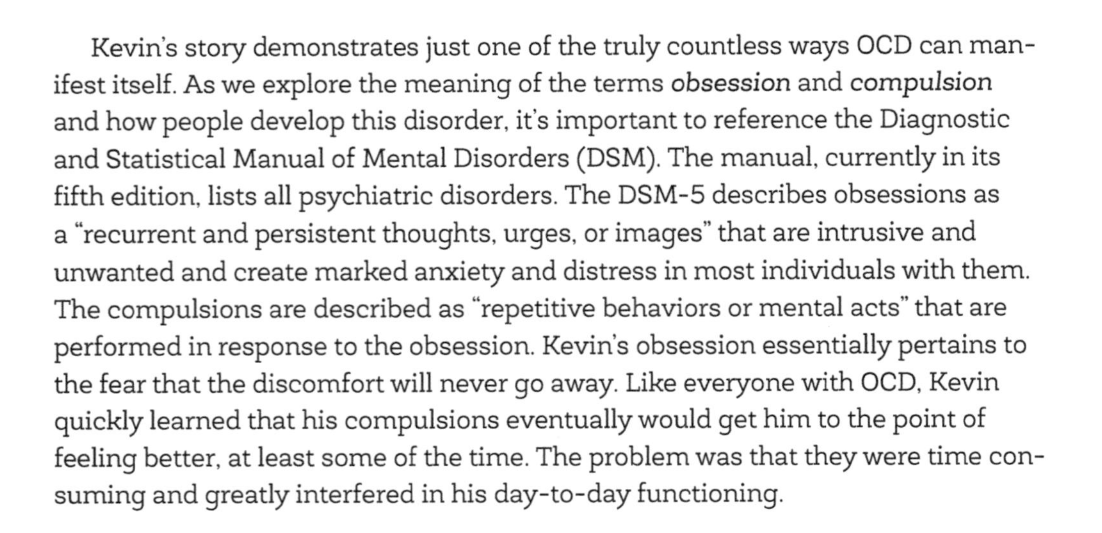

Kevin's story demonstrates just one of the truly countless ways OCD can manifest itself. As we explore the meaning of the terms *obsession* and *compulsion* and how people develop this disorder, it's important to reference the Diagnostic and Statistical Manual of Mental Disorders (DSM). The manual, currently in its fifth edition, lists all psychiatric disorders. The DSM-5 describes obsessions as a "recurrent and persistent thoughts, urges, or images" that are intrusive and unwanted and create marked anxiety and distress in most individuals with them. The compulsions are described as "repetitive behaviors or mental acts" that are performed in response to the obsession. Kevin's obsession essentially pertains to the fear that the discomfort will never go away. Like everyone with OCD, Kevin quickly learned that his compulsions eventually would get him to the point of feeling better, at least some of the time. The problem was that they were time consuming and greatly interfered in his day-to-day functioning.

Neurological Effects

Do we know what causes OCD? The short answer is not really. However, we do have some good ideas based on research. Abnormalities in brain functioning appear to play some role. The frontal cortex and subcortical structures of the brain may be different in people with OCD than in people without it, according to the National Institute of Mental Health. Additionally, it's widely accepted that the neurotransmitter serotonin may not be performing properly. This is why the use of selective serotonin reuptake inhibitor (SSRI) medications is the first-line treatment for OCD.

OCD is also believed to run in families. There is a 10 to 20 percent greater risk of developing the disorder if a parent or sibling already has it, according to a study published in *Psychiatric Clinics of North America*, which looked at the genetic aspects of OCD. Keep in mind, however, that even though the incidence of developing OCD is higher if a parent or sibling already has it, there is still a greater likelihood that someone won't.

Heredity isn't the only cause of OCD. Pediatric autoimmune neuropsychiatric disorder associated with streptococcus (PANDAS) and pediatric acute-onset neuropsychiatric syndrome (PANS) are also known causes of the disorder. Both result from infections that cause inflammation in the child's brain. PANDAS is caused by a strep infection in children while PANS occurs as a result of other infections, such as mycoplasma, chicken pox, Lyme disease, and mononucleosis.

BY THE NUMBERS

It's difficult to know exactly how many people have OCD, but the International OCD Foundation estimates that OCD affects approximately 1 in 100 adults and 1 in 200 children. That translates to about 2 to 3 million adults and 500,000 children. The IOCDF also indicates that OCD typically occurs during one of two developmental periods, the first being between the ages of 8 and 12, and the other being from the late teenage years to the early twenties. OCD can first occur earlier in childhood and later in adulthood, though instances of such are not as common. These numbers clearly demonstrate that OCD is not the rare disorder it was once believed to be.

For children who have either PANDAS or PANS, it's believed that the OCD develops quickly. If you are concerned that your child's OCD may be a result of either, it is recommended that you consult with your pediatrician or a child psychiatrist, as thorough medical testing is needed to assess for the presence of either condition.

Trauma may play some role as well, according to a 2007 study published in *Behaviour Research and Therapy*, although I've seen very few cases in my practice. Stress itself doesn't generally seem to cause OCD, though it can certainly contribute to the onset of the disorder and exacerbate symptoms in someone who already has it.

Most people reading this book likely already know how overwhelming it is to live with OCD. For some, the disorder can bring about feelings of depression or even suicide. If you are having thoughts of suicide or self-harm in any way (or any other emergent mental health issue), please stop reading this book right now and immediately seek medical attention. Go immediately to your local hospital emergency room for assistance. Your safety needs to be the first priority. This book will still be there when you return home.

Expressions of OCD

Many years ago, OCD was a little-known disorder. Today, most people now have at least some understanding of it; probably the most well-known behaviors include compulsive handwashing and checking items such as ovens and doors. Yet there are many other manifestations that are also important to recognize. As we discuss the various forms of OCD, consider the term itself: obsessive-compulsive disorder. In order for the diagnosis to be made, people need to experience unwanted thoughts and images as well as some compulsive action in response to those feelings.

Before I go any further, I want to recognize that there is an obsessional form of OCD referred to as "pure O." The theory is that some people may exhibit obsessions without showing signs of compulsive behaviors. Most specialists don't believe this theory, but understand the reasoning behind it. I'm one of those specialists. My thought process is that just because we can't see a compulsion, it doesn't mean that it's not present. As an example, let's say someone has fears of harm coming to a family member, and as a result they engage in repetitive praying. We can't see that compulsion, but it certainly counts as one.

Perhaps even more confusing is when someone tries to "outsmart" the OCD. An example would be someone has a thought that they may have acted in an inappropriate sexual manner and can't quite remember the details of what happened. They don't truly believe that it happened, but they're also not 100 percent sure of that. As a result, they replay the situation over and over in their mind to try to find some explanation that allows them to feel some semblance of reassurance that nothing happened. That repetitive thought reaction needs to be thought of as a compulsion. So, while I do understand the term "pure O," I don't think that it actually exists.

One of the most challenging aspects in treating OCD is how the disorder expresses itself; no two people have it in the exact same way. The manifestations of OCD are truly endless, but we can categorize them. I've already mentioned a

ON MEDICATION

Many people who have OCD will benefit from taking medication. In fact, the best treatment for most is a combination of medication and a very specific form of cognitive behavioral therapy (CBT) called ERP therapy. The latter will be discussed in great detail later in this book.

The first-line drugs used to treat OCD are usually SSRIs. This specific class of drugs works on the neurotransmitter serotonin, which is believed to play a role in the development of obsessions and compulsions. Celexa, Lexapro, Luvox, Paxil, Prozac, and Zoloft are all equally effective. As a licensed clinical social worker, I do not prescribe medication, but I am often in the position of recommending to my patients that they see a doctor who can. This can be done by both a psychiatrist and a primary care physician.

Taking medication is a very personal decision. I know many people are reluctant to do so. Misconceptions about what medication might actually do and the belief that taking medications is a sign of weakness are typical reasons that people choose to avoid this line of treatment. I can only say that I've known many people who initially resisted medication then, once they started, wished the treatment had begun sooner. The relief that the medication eventually brought them was well worth it.

few—contamination, harm, and "just right" OCD. Another very common obsession revolves around doubtfulness. This often occurs when someone can't recall if a particular action has been completed. Is a door locked? Is the oven off? Do they have their phone or keys with them? This sense of doubt often triggers the checking compulsions. It's not usual to see someone with this type of OCD and fear turn around and drive right back so they can make sure that the front door is locked or the garage door is closed—even if they're miles from home.

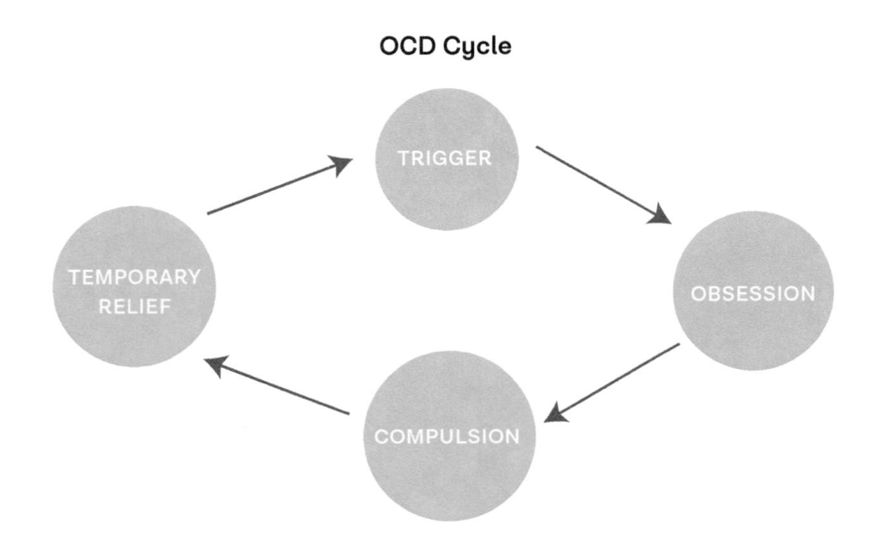

FIGURE 1.1 *OCD episodes always begin with a trigger. Common examples are touching something believed to be dirty or simply having some intrusive, random thought about harming someone. This trigger quickly leads to obsessive thoughts. The compulsive behavior follows and frequently does serve to lessen the distress and anxiety caused by the trigger. However, relief is only temporary; another trigger will restart the cycle.*

Symmetry, orderliness, and counting are also common manifestations of OCD. Symmetry and orderliness can be seen when items must be lined up in a certain way. For example, in the refrigerator all bottles and cans must be put in a way so that the labels face out, or books in a bookcase have to be organized by their height. Counting can occur with almost anything. A person must count the stairs each time they walk up and down them, or while reading they count every letter *T* they come across. Interestingly, the obsessional thinking associated with these types of actions can also be endless. One might assume that the usual obsession with these types of actions may be about trying to ward off some harm or dreaded event from occurring. But it may also be the "just right" OCD, when a person feels compelled to engage in a repetitive action until they feel some sense of completion.

Before moving on, I do want to say a word about hoarding, which will not be referred to in this book in much detail. In prior editions of the DSM, OCD had been classified as an anxiety disorder. In DSM-5, a new category of OCD and Related Disorders was added, which includes body dysmorphic disorder (obsessions associated with physical appearance), trichotillomania (hair pulling disorder), excoriation (skin picking disorder), and hoarding disorder.

This change came as a result of recognizing that these disorders share many characteristics with OCD but are also different enough to warrant their own diagnosis. In hoarding, the key obsessional element is the fear of losing something believed to be of value, and the key compulsive action is the hoarding behavior itself. Treatment, though, is very different from the more classic forms of OCD. Given the new DSM-5 classification of hoarding and the differences in treatment, I felt it best to keep the focus of this book instead on OCD itself. Please refer to the Resources (page 129) in the back of this book for helpful information specific to hoarding.

How This Book Can Help

Kevin, the teenager mentioned earlier, is doing great. Sure, his obsessive thoughts still pop up, but he is able to dismiss them fairly easily. He has learned that if he disengages from his compulsions, the urge to do them will subside. He is still triggered at times enough to perform his rituals associated with light switches and doors. Sometimes when walking, he still gets an urge to have to repeat his steps. But Kevin has learned how to frustrate and confuse the OCD. With regard to his urge to walk back and forth over cracks three times and turn his head to the right, Kevin has it much more under control. Sometimes he doesn't complete the compulsion at all, and other times he goes back only once or twice. He's learned to turn his head to the left or not at all. All of his effort to weaken the OCD has worked. The disorder doesn't control him much anymore. Kevin also now knows that when he resists those urges, the OCD is going to push back and try to make him feel that there is something very important about performing those compulsions. He understands that if he fights back, the OCD will eventually relent.

SPECIAL SECTION: OCD SYMPTOM CHECKLIST

Below is a list containing many of the recognized obsessions and compulsions. As you'll see, some are well known while others you may be learning about for the first time. You may also discover that you're struggling with some forms OCD you didn't previously recognize. Please select those you feel you are experiencing. As you work through this book, knowing which of these you want to address will help you in deciding which type of therapeutic intervention to use.

AGGRESSIVE OBSESSIONS

- ☐ Fear of harming oneself.
- ☐ Fear of harming others.
- ☐ Intrusive violent images.
- ☐ Fear of causing harm due to your own inaction—i.e., not wiping up water found on stairs, which someone could slip on.
- ☐ Fear of hitting someone/an animal while driving.
- ☐ Fear of suddenly losing control and saying something offensive to someone.
- ☐ Fear of writing something offensive.

CONTAMINATION OBSESSIONS

- ☐ Fear of dirt, germs, bodily waste.
- ☐ Fear of environmental contaminants, such as lead, asbestos, radiation, mold.
- ☐ Fear of blood.
- ☐ Fear of household items such as insect spray, bleach, cleaners, furniture polish.
- ☐ Fear of uncooked food items; fear of salmonella, E. coli.
- ☐ Fear of diseases, such as AIDS, Ebola, cancer.
- ☐ Fear of animals and fear of catching rabies.
- ☐ Contamination obsessions may also contribute to the development of somatic obsessions associated with illness.

RELIGIOUS OBSESSIONS

- ☐ Fear of having blasphemous thoughts and doing something against one's religious values.
- ☐ Fear of screaming out blasphemous statements while in a place of worship.
- ☐ Fear of being punished by God for "bad" thoughts.
- ☐ Fear of using God's name in anger.
- ☐ Fear of seeing something red or the number 666.

SCRUPULOSITY

- ☐ Similar to religious obsessions, but focus instead is on concerns related to morality and ethical behavior.

SEXUAL OBSESSIONS

- ☐ Fear of having thoughts about children that are believed to be sexual in nature.
- ☐ Experiencing sexual sensations/arousal in circumstances considered inappropriate, such as in the presence of children.
- ☐ Fear of losing control and engaging in sexual behavior with children.
- ☐ Similar thoughts about family members/animals.

- ☐ Fear of becoming homosexual when person believes they are heterosexual (referred to as HOCD). Certainly, the opposite can be true when someone who is gay has fears of becoming heterosexual.

HOARDING AND SAVING

- ☐ The essence of this obsession is the fear of losing something believed to be of value. The item(s) often may appear as useless to others.
- ☐ There is no limit as to the type of items that can be hoarded, though newspapers, magazines, old clothes, and shopping bags are among the most common.

SYMMETRY AND EXACTNESS

- ☐ Items have to be placed in a certain manner or direction. This could include, for example, books in a bookcase, bottles in a refrigerator, or clothing all being folded in the same way.
- ☐ Need to engage in certain behaviors, such as writing, in a very specific manner.

CHECKING COMPULSIONS

- ☐ Examples include doors, windows, locks, ovens, stove tops, smartphones (whether they are on or off).
- ☐ Checking that you did not harm others or that you will not harm yourself.
- ☐ Checking that you didn't insult someone.
- ☐ Checking for bodily sensations as indicators of illness.
- ☐ Excessive checking of lists.
- ☐ Checking contents in pockets, bags, purses, wallets, backpacks, etc.
- ☐ Checking that items are where you believe they are supposed to be.
- ☐ Checking that a mistake was not made, such as with homework.

CLEANING AND WASHING COMPULSIONS

- ☐ Handwashing, excessive and/or ritualized.
- ☐ Excessive and/or ritualized behaviors associated with hygiene, such as showering, bathing, brushing teeth, and wiping after toilet use.
- ☐ Cleaning of inanimate objects, including smartphones.
- ☐ Excessive use of hand sanitizer and wipes.

REPEATING AND COUNTING RITUALS

- ☐ Often associated with walking, touching, tapping, rubbing, reading, and writing.
- ☐ Almost anything can be counted: steps, words, ceiling tiles, seconds on a clock.
- ☐ Rewinding TV shows, videos, DVR.

MISCELLANEOUS OBSESSIONS AND COMPULSIONS

- ☐ "The need to know." This is basically a form of checking. An example could be stopping to identify items seen while walking.
- ☐ "Just right" OCD, as was discussed earlier in this chapter. ▶

OCD Symptom Checklist, continued

- ☐ Sensorimotor OCD (aka hyperawareness OCD). This occurs when someone can't stop thinking about normal, automatic bodily sensations, such as blinking, swallowing, breathing, their heartbeat, and tongue and mouth movements. Being hyperaware of making eye contact with others, floaters in the eyes, and body movements such as arms and legs while walking all are known manifestations of this form of OCD.
- ☐ Relationship OCD. This pertains to obsessional thinking over a relationship. Common thoughts often are associated with fears that the person may not truly love their partner or that the partner doesn't really want to be with them.
- ☐ Existential OCD. Examples of this may be obsessions over the meaning of life and reality.
- ☐ Mental rituals, such as praying or having to say certain phrases.
- ☐ Obsessive slowness. The better term is probably *compulsive slowness*, as this occurs when someone takes a long time to complete routine tasks, such as bathing, brushing teeth, and getting dressed.
- ☐ Emotional contamination. This pertains to the fear of essentially picking up qualities of other people found to be either frightening or disturbing in some way. One example could be obsessions over becoming homeless after having seen a homeless person.
- ☐ Reassurance seeking. In my opinion, this is the most common compulsion of all. Typically, reassurance seeking occurs when there is a fear of something bad happening. Examples could be the fear of harm coming to someone, doing poorly on a test, or becoming ill. If getting reassurance actually worked, people wouldn't feel the need to do it so often.

WORKING THROUGH HARM OR SEXUAL OBSESSIONS

These types of obsessions are often the most disturbing for someone with OCD and sometimes even for their therapists. I have found this especially true for clinicians who have little experience with the disorder. All therapists are required to report cases of suspected abuse, and some may understandably worry when they hear a patient acknowledge having these types of thoughts. However, in this circumstance we're referring to OCD, which means that the person is at little or no risk of actually causing harm. In fact, I've never come across someone with this type of OCD who has ever acted on their thoughts. However, with these cases, I am always careful to conduct a risk assessment. If I've never met someone before, I don't know whether they would do something terrible or not but it's not that difficult to make that assessment. Consider these questions:

1. Does the person enjoy having these thoughts? If they struggle with OCD, the obvious answer is no (they also probably wouldn't come to see me in the first place if they did enjoy them).

2. Is the person *trying* to have these thoughts? Again, with OCD the answer is going to be no. This shouldn't be confused with the compulsive mental act of trying to figure them out—that is purposeful.

3. Does the person have a prior history of acting out in this way? If the answer is no, this is probably another sign that we're dealing with OCD. If the answer is yes, then I need to know more about those circumstances before I can be sure that the symptoms warrant an OCD diagnosis.

4. Is the person actively psychotic? If the answer is yes, then I wouldn't treat such thoughts as OCD.

If these questions have been sufficiently addressed and it's been determined that these thoughts, images, and urges are OCD related, then it's time to work toward exposure therapy. I've seen so many people with these types of obsessions over the years and haven't found any to be at risk of causing any harm to themselves or anyone else. I can't say with 100 percent certainty that it will never happen. But I can say that the likelihood is so low that it doesn't warrant all the torment and life disruption that comes with it.

Now it's your turn. What are your symptoms? How would you classify yourself? The preceding list is by no means an exhaustive one. Did you see any of your own obsessions and compulsions? If so, which ones did you identify with mostly? Did I miss any? Please write those down as well in the space below:

____

____

____

____

____

____

Both Kevin and his parents have learned that our goal was never to fully eliminate the OCD. Much research has been conducted on the disorder and continues to be, but a cure for OCD has yet to be discovered. To many, that can be very disappointing news, but it's something people have to learn to accept at this point in time. The current goal in treating OCD is management. Life requires people to manage many things, and for some OCD is one of them.

My goal for you as you read this book is that you, too, have a similar experience to Kevin's. OCD is determined; it doesn't give up easily. As we go forward in this book, we will take a much deeper look at how OCD is treated, with a special emphasis on ERP. Please know that OCD may not give up easily, but ERP is equally tough. This therapy gives people the necessary tools to manage OCD. It's not an easy process, but as you've likely heard before, things that are worth doing often aren't. ERP will challenge you, frustrate you, and at times even scare you. But we'll do it together and in ways that feel manageable and respectful. As I tell my patients, it's never my goal to scare the daylights out of them. We're just trying to beat the OCD into submission. As Kevin once said to me, "I know OCD is going to win sometimes, but I'm going to win more." The ultimate goal, of course, is improving your quality of life. Kevin is doing well in high school; he can now go out with friends and participate in sports without the OCD dictating his next move. I wouldn't have written this book if I didn't feel the same could be true for people who choose to read it.

Wrap-Up

We've covered a lot so far in this first chapter. You've gotten to know Kevin and his struggles as well as his successes in dealing with OCD. You've learned about the DSM-5 and possible causes for the disorder. Additionally, we've described the many forms OCD can take and introduced treatment options, especially medication and ERP. There's so much more to come. As was mentioned earlier, the focus will be on helping you develop a treatment plan as we move forward.

As you have seen both from this book and from your own personal experiences, OCD is very creative. People often ask me if I've ever heard of their form of OCD. Usually the answer is yes, but sometimes I hear about obsessions and compulsions I've never encountered before. What's important to know is that it doesn't matter. Sure, I need to know as much as I can to develop an effective plan, but truth be told, all forms of OCD are unusual. That's the nature of the disorder.

What's important is that we stick to what works and think carefully about how to apply the exposure therapy protocol to fit your specific needs. As creative as OCD is, we need to be even more creative.

I encourage you to check in with yourself after each chapter. Assess how you're feeling and what you've learned. Of course, reading a book like this isn't like reading a novel. Take some time to think about what you've read, and go back to parts that you feel you need to review more. This is a lot of information to take in.

So, how's this going for you so far? Do you feel that you've learned anything new? About yourself? About OCD? Have you identified areas you feel you need to work on more? As we move forward to focus on treatment, what are you looking forward to? Are you worried or frightened? That's normal and to be expected. Please, make note of that, too.

CHAPTER TWO

Therapeutic Approaches

UNLIKE SOME OTHER PSYCHIATRIC PROBLEMS, there is little debate as to which approaches are most effective for OCD. The treatment of choice is typically CBT. But that concept is really too broad of a term to truly describe the recommended approach for OCD. Imaginal exposure and ERP are forms of behavioral therapy, but they offer more specifically defined treatment. ACT and mindfulness can also be used, though more often they are considered adjunct approaches that can provide some relief. All will be described here.

Primary Treatment Methods

According to the International OCD Foundation, once someone begins showing symptoms of OCD, it takes an average of 14 to 17 years before they receive appropriate treatment. With all that is known about OCD at this point, how can that still be possible? One reason may be due to a critical shortage of clinicians skilled in assessing and treating OCD. I believe many patients wind up getting misdiagnosed and/or receiving ineffective treatment.

This may seem odd, but if you have to have OCD, there's never been a better time to have it. In recent years, research and advances in medications and therapy have made great strides in treating the disorder. A diagnosis of OCD today means there is a far greater likelihood of getting better than ever before.

Cognitive Behavioral Therapy

The essence of CBT is really what the term itself implies. The cognitive piece is about building awareness of your distorted negative thinking patterns, and the behavioral part is about confronting the maladaptive coping strategies by utilizing a variety of very specific techniques. Keep in mind that distorted thinking patterns are not unique to OCD. We all experience such thoughts regardless of whether we have a psychiatric problem or not. The power of the cognitive therapy part of CBT lies in learning to think from a more rational perspective and developing more effective ways to diminish your distress.

Exposure and Response Prevention Therapy

A 2015 report published in *Psychiatry Research* on the efficacy of CBT for treating OCD stated that "in light of the abundance of evidence supporting the application of ERP, this treatment should be predominant in first-line evidence-based psychological interventions for OCD."

If you have a phobia of elevators, the best treatment is to get in an elevator. The same thinking applies to treating OCD. If you're fearful of germs and engage in all sorts of compulsive acts to avoid contact with them, your therapy plan is going to include exposure to situations that frighten you. This could mean touching doorknobs with bare hands, or perhaps shaking hands with someone with whom you might ordinarily avoid contact. There are many examples of this when it comes to OCD therapy.

As I mentioned in chapter 1, ERP is conducted in a step-by-step manner to increase your chances of success and to build your confidence. If you have a phobia of elevators, the first exposure wouldn't be to get in an elevator and go up 20 floors. Instead you might be assigned first to get in the elevator and walk out before the door even closes. Once your anxiety associated with that sufficiently subsides, you would then move on to subsequent items on your hierarchy and continue doing that until you eventually get to the point of being able to go up to the twentieth floor. The same incremental approach is used for OCD.

But with ERP, it's not enough to be exposed to your fears. The therapy also calls for a response prevention plan after the exposure. This means not performing the related compulsive behavior associated with the obsession. Maybe you've taken that first step and touched something you believe to be contaminated; now you need to stop the compulsion that drives you to clean your hands afterward. If you're working on checking behaviors associated with the stove top, you must start to resist the compulsion to check the burners. If you're doing exposure work but not also doing the response prevention, then you're not really engaging in ERP.

Imaginal Exposure

Imaginal exposure is another form of ERP therapy, but instead of real-life situations it uses imagery. This is a wonderfully effective technique for many forms of OCD, especially for those wherein real-life exposure may be especially difficult, impractical, or even inappropriate. A good example is if someone has fears of losing control at an airport and screaming, "I have a gun!" For such an obsessive thought, I might write a story, usually referred to as an exposure script, that involves this very event occurring. The person then reads the story over and over again or perhaps records and then listens to it repeatedly until the anxiety and fear subside. This can be a very powerful technique, provided that the script itself produces enough anxiety to make the exposure worthwhile. We will review this technique in much more detail later.

Digging In to CBT

Here's a situation most of us have been in at least once in our lives: Let's say you're about to be interviewed for a job, and you're sitting patiently in the waiting room. You look up and see the door to the interview room open; the supervisor exits with another candidate, and they appear to have had a great time. They're laughing and shaking hands, and you hear the supervisor say, "We'll be in touch." You've watched all this unfold in front of you. What thoughts do you think would go through your head at this time? If you thought, *I don't stand a chance*, you're in good company.

I often give this example to the classes that I teach, and that reaction is by far the most common given by the students. Other popular reactions include *Why should I even bother?* and *The other person got the job*. These are all variations of the same theme: feeling defeated before the interview even begins.

On a more positive note, I've heard people say the scenario gives them hope that they'll have an equally good experience. Others have expressed that it makes them feel challenged to try hard in the interview. Some people have suggested that the supervisor and candidate already knew each other, and the supervisor was being polite. You can see through this one interaction how our automatic thoughts—negative and positive—can shape how we feel and, in turn, our behavior. Thoughts, feelings, behaviors—CBT is about learning how each affects the other and how to utilize a variety of strategies that help promote more realistic thinking and eliminate disruptive patterns of behavior.

It's important to think of *CBT* as an umbrella term. There are several approaches that involve principles of CBT, and ERP is one of them. Let's break down the acronym to get a better understanding of the concept. The *C* stands for cognitive therapy, which promotes alternate ways of thinking. Typically, a person with automatic negative thought patterns, the primary contributing factor to emotional distress, is taught to consider a different perspective. Some people make the mistake of thinking of CBT as simply positive thinking. In actuality it's about thinking more rationally. Now, let's turn to the behavioral part.

The *B* in CBT is about taking action to address a problem. Behavior therapy comes in many forms. For OCD it means doing ERP therapy. For people who pull their hair or pick their skin it means using habit reversal training (HRT). When it comes to panic attacks it may involve what's called "interoceptive exposure," or purposely bringing on panic-related symptoms such as light-headedness, to prove the person can cope with the uncomfortable sensation. Meditation, deep breathing, and progressive muscle relaxation all can be considered behavioral techniques. Deciding on which technique to use depends on which problem we're trying to address.

ADJUNCTIVE APPROACHES: MINDFULNESS AND ACCEPTANCE AND COMMITMENT THERAPY

The practice of mindfulness has been around for centuries. With OCD, mindfulness can teach you how to be present with disturbing thoughts without giving them any significance. As was discussed earlier, the more you try to rationalize your obsessions, the more trouble the OCD will cause. It's easy to fall into the OCD trap of trying to figure out reasons why the thoughts shouldn't bother you. Usually, when you think you've found the answer, the OCD pops up and forces you to reconsider your rationale. Consider what your OCD might say if it could talk. Perhaps something like, "Yeah, but have you thought of this?"

Take, for example, a person who has the type of obsessive thoughts mentioned earlier, pertaining to shouting "I have a gun" at an airport. A mindfulness exercise associated with this could simply be noticing the thoughts, then focusing instead on their breathing. Learning mindfulness techniques can help you develop the capacity to stay in the moment, observe whatever you're experiencing, and accept your thoughts without placing any judgments on yourself for having them. You can learn to disengage from trying to figure out your thoughts. Sounds terrific, doesn't it? It's also very hard work. It takes practice and patience, but the outcomes are worthwhile. We will explore this in more detail a little later.

Acceptance and commitment therapy (ACT) offers additional help for people working to develop the skill to accept the obsessive thoughts without trying to change them. This protocol calls for people to understand that their thoughts are considered neither good nor bad. The idea is to take your thoughts at face value, then take some actions toward building a life that is consistent with your own set of values. In essence, we can have obsessions while also engaging in life in meaningful ways.

A primary goal of exposure-based therapy for OCD is to reduce anxiety while disengaging from compulsions. ACT also works toward that goal, though with differing techniques. It encourages people to accept their obsessions as random thoughts and to find ways to continue to live life even though the distress may still be present. The uncomfortable thoughts, images, or urges all may be there, but you can still work, go to school, have relationships, and do whatever else is important to you. According to a 2013 study published in *Journal of Cognitive Psychotherapy* that compared the exposure and acceptance of obsession thoughts, "ACT seeks to change one's relationship with obsessional thoughts and anxiety by increasing the patient's willingness to accept these experiences as part of the normal human experience, see them as your thoughts, and continue pursuing one's values."

What do you think? Are these new concepts to you? Have you seen them before? As you write your thoughts below, please include how you feel about engaging in these techniques and any trepidations you may have about doing so.

Maintaining Mindfulness

Earlier in my career, I taught a stress management class for the Palo Alto Medical Foundation. The people who attended had a variety of health conditions, such as chronic pain, high blood pressure, irritable bowel syndrome, insomnia, depression and anxiety, and numerous other medical and psychological issues. Before I received training to facilitate the workshop, I had little experience with mindfulness and frankly relied on the more traditional forms of therapy to treat anxiety disorders. While I became skilled in the various techniques associated with CBT, I paid little attention to the potential benefits of mindfulness. I now see the tremendous relief it can bring people who have various psychiatric illnesses, including OCD. I wouldn't say that I completely discounted mindfulness, but I didn't see the point of using it when so much research supported other evidence-based treatment. I now believe that mindfulness for OCD can be very beneficial when used together with CBT.

Before turning to the benefits of mindfulness for OCD, I'd like to address the usefulness of mindfulness with various medical and stress-related conditions. In his 2009 study on the benefits of mindfulness, published in *Complementary Health Practice Review*, Dr. Jeffrey Greeson states that "the ability to simply observe and accurately sense thoughts, emotions, and physical sensations—without having to change them, or act on them—can be instrumental in breaking habitual behavior patterns that can harm one's health, such as smoking a cigarette when feeling stressed, eating comfort food when feeling sad or 'empty,' or turning to alcohol or other substances to 'numb out' when feeling overwhelmed."

Furthermore, he cited several other articles indicating that mindfulness has been shown to be beneficial for those suffering from various medical conditions, such as type 1 diabetes, chronic pain, lower back pain, hypertension, myocardial ischemia, irritable bowel syndrome, insomnia, and HIV. Additionally, mindfulness is known to help lessen mood-related problems, such as depression, and to ease stress and anxiety. On the whole, people who consistently practice mindfulness can achieve a greater overall sense of emotional well-being and learn to better cope with acute and chronic medical and emotional problems. Seems like a good idea to me.

As we discussed earlier, mindfulness can be a very useful adjunct strategy in treating OCD. The key is to try to accept that the obsessions are simply thoughts. The emphasis is on observing them and staying focused on whatever mindfulness exercises you may use. As people learn to do this effectively, they begin recognizing that their obsessive thoughts have no real power and are of no real significance. In fact, all they really mean is that you have OCD. I've seen mindfulness be especially helpful in people whose obsessive thoughts continue to resurface and their ERP exercises can't provide relief. Similarly, I have found that people who have sensorimotor OCD, with the emphasis on automatic bodily functions, such as breathing, blinking, and swallowing, benefit from mindfulness strategies. The practice teaches them how to disengage from the frustrations associated with paying so much attention to these sensations. In a discussion of mindfulness for OCD, Dr. Clara Strauss, a clinical psychologist in the UK, said mindfulness "therapy encourages patients to attend non-judgmentally to their intrusive thoughts, increase their acceptance of physical sensations of anxiety, and bring greater awareness to urges to engage in compulsive [behaviors]."

Many clients have told me that they've tried mindfulness and that it didn't work for them, only to later learn that they either weren't really engaging in mindfulness or didn't put enough time into truly getting good at it. You'll have the chance to try some mindfulness exercises yourself later on in an upcoming chapter. While I realize it's not for everyone, what do you think? Do you see some benefit in it for yourself? If yes, take a moment to write your thoughts down here, and if not, also write those thoughts down as well.

____

____

____

____

____

____

____

Exposure and Response Prevention

When it comes to OCD, I use much more behavior therapy than I do cognitive therapy. I often say, "The proof is in the doing." Many if not most people who have OCD have fairly good insight about what they're going through. They generally know that what they're thinking and what they're doing as a result doesn't actually make much sense, but they're unable to control it. For example, I have yet to meet someone with harm obsessions who has told me that they want to harm anyone. It's usually the exact opposite. Even though they've experienced thousands of harm-related thoughts without ever acting on them, knowing that truth doesn't stop their obsession. A main component of cognitive therapy is to look at evidence that supports a person's negative thoughts, then to examine evidence that suggests that these thoughts may not be true, all in an attempt to promote more rational thinking.

I remember once meeting with a patient who had a terrible fear of hitting someone with his car, which is often referred to as "hit-and-run" OCD. One day I asked him how many times he had been in his car over the past week, and he said 10. I asked him how many times he hit someone, and he told me zero times. We then made similar estimates for a month and a year. By the time we got to 10 years, he estimated that he had driven about 5,000 times and never hit a person. At this point I usually ask the big question: "What does that tell you?" My hope is that that someone will see there isn't much evidence to support their fear and stop worrying so much about it. What do I hear is "well, I guess it's more likely to happen now," or "it just hasn't happened yet."

As I said earlier, the proof to treating the disorder is in the doing. A person with "hit-and-run" OCD is likely going to have to get in the car and drive in areas that trigger the obsession, and only then will they begin to believe that the odds of nothing bad happening are truly on their side. Over the years, I've learned that I'm not likely to talk someone out of their obsessive fears. They're going to have to prove it to themselves, and that typically means doing the exposure therapy.

When I teach on OCD, I always do some exposure exercises in class. I find it's the best way to learn how to actually do ERP. So, let's try an ERP exercise. Take a moment to touch the bottom of your shoe, provided that you haven't just stepped in something someone without OCD might consider worrisome. Please don't feel pressured to do this if you're not feeling ready. We will explore ERP in much more detail later. If you are ready, give it a go.

Be careful not to just touch your shoe with your fingertip or cup your hand around the sole so you don't actually touch the bottom. In order for this to be effective, you have to touch it. Thoroughly. No shortcuts.

How do you feel now? I would expect that there would be some discomfort, even for someone without contamination fears. It bothers me, too. It's gross. But is it dangerous? I don't think so, unless you've stepped in toxic chemicals. Now, with that same hand, rub the bottom of your shoe again, and this time place your hand on your face and rub your face with that same hand. Still pretty disgusting, right? It is for me, too.

OK, the first step is done. You've done the exposure part, now comes the response prevention: no handwashing, no using hand sanitizer, and no rubbing your hands on some other object in an attempt to decontaminate. Now touch other objects at home with those hands, including furniture, clothes, plates, cups, and even other family members. Get everything good and dirty. How much anxiety are you experiencing now? Wait a little while, then assess your level of anxiety again. How about in 10 minutes? How about after 30 minutes? One hour? Have you noticed that time is on your side? The more time that passes without doing the compulsions mentioned previously, the more likely it is that the anxiety will fade. It has to—no one stays anxious forever.

Exposure Therapy Cycle (ERP)

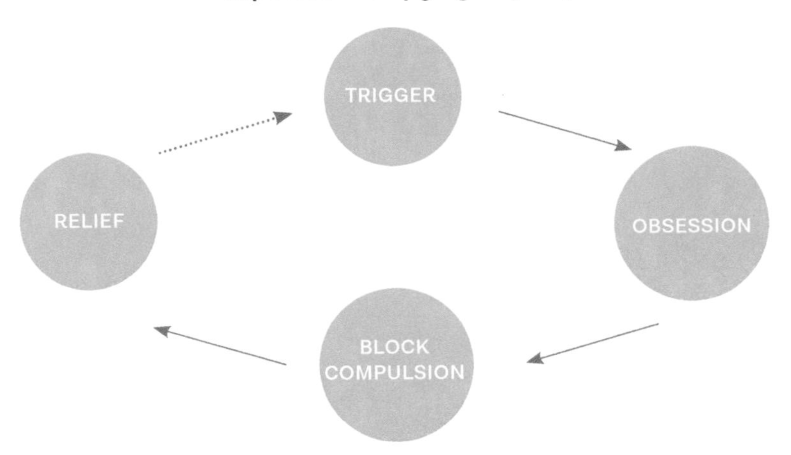

FIGURE 2.1 *The ERP cycle still begins with a trigger, but now we need to prevent the compulsion from happening. For the ERP process to work, it must cause some anxiety. If the compulsion is resisted long enough, the urge to act on it will subside.*

MANAGING DISCOMFORT

Managing the discomfort caused by ERP is an interesting and somewhat controversial topic. Done properly, this therapy and the subsequent work toward eliminating compulsive actions will cause anxious feelings for a while. It makes sense. Removing the compulsions takes away the very action that's used to manage the discomfort. This usually leaves a very important question: How does someone deal with all of these uncomfortable feelings that this process brings?

It depends on whom you ask. Many OCD experts view relaxation exercises and meditation as means to avoid anxiety. If the goal is to learn that the anxiety can't hurt you, then these relaxation techniques are viewed as counterproductive. On the other hand, some experts see the goal of OCD treatment as learning how to manage anxiety. So why not use these exercises to get to that point?

Frankly, I'm a fan of what works for each individual I treat. I do use some relaxation techniques, such as deep breathing and progressive muscle relaxation if the anxiety caused by ERP feels unmanageable. I do prefer to let my patient sit with their anxiety, as I believe those feelings will lessen as the compulsions aren't acted upon. If the anxiety doesn't subside, it may mean that we've selected an ERP exercise the person isn't ready for yet. If that's the case, we need to do a different exposure that doesn't provoke as much anxiety, then revisit the other exercise when the person is ready.

Imaginal Exposure in Detail

As was mentioned earlier, imaginal exposure can be a very effective form of treatment for OCD—if the steps are implemented correctly. In order to work, it must invoke anxiety. If it doesn't, the process is pointless.

Here's an exercise that many of my students find troubling, and they usually don't have OCD themselves. If you are willing, try this exercise, which explains a way to do exposure with harm-related thoughts. Think of the name of someone close to you: spouse, child, parent, or close friend. Now, write this sentence: "Someday I'm going to lose control and kill [the person's name]." How much anxiety do you feel now? On a scale of 1 to 10, with 10 being panic-level anxiety, rate how you're feeling. Now, write that sentence over and over for five minutes straight. What's your anxiety level now? How about after ten minutes? Thirty minutes? During the exercise, you can also embellish how you might commit this act. Would you run someone over with a car or use a knife? How about thinking about pushing the person onto train tracks? Feel more anxious now? Good. This is important.

The concept behind this type of exposure is that someone with OCD already has these types of thoughts, so why not prompt them on purpose? Avoiding them doesn't work, and in fact doing so can make these types of thoughts feel even stronger. Yes, these are often gruesome thoughts, but keep in mind that the goal of therapy is not to eliminate them. Many people without OCD have these types of thoughts. But most don't pay much attention to them since they know they'd never act on them. The thoughts just come and go with little fanfare.

But if you're someone with OCD, these thoughts get stuck in your head, and you begin to wonder what they may mean about you. You get scared and may try to prevent yourself from even having them, which causes them to get stronger and your fear to become even more intense. Even if you don't have a history of harming another person, knowing that still doesn't bring any reassurance. The OCD will just twist it another way and try to tell you that as time goes on it becomes even more likely you will perform the harmful acts.

The goal of therapy is to get to the point where these types of thoughts can occur, but they cause little if any distress. I do recognize that these types of thoughts, as well as those about being a child molester, are among the most troubling thoughts some people with OCD experience. The disorder often targets what the person holds most dear. If being nonviolent, for example, is a particularly important value to you, these may be precisely the types of thoughts that will surface. OCD can be very cruel like that. I don't have OCD myself, but I recall once being in a department store and seeing a woman come toward me who was pregnant. The thought of punching her in the stomach suddenly flashed in my head. She walked past me, and that was that. I use it as an example to tell people in my OCD group that most people do in fact have such thoughts and generally forget about them.

Making the Commitment

People sometimes tell me that they don't have the willpower to participate in exposure therapy. I don't see willpower as the issue holding them back. OCD is a psychiatric illness and a powerful one at that. It makes people worry about things that usually make little sense and often tacks on a heavy dose of shame. Exposure therapy is about doing the work and sticking with it—even when it all seems so overwhelming. Studies show that most people who do exposure therapy will get better (Osborn, 1998). It's also well known that OCD doesn't give up without a fight. Some days it's going to knock you down, but your job is to get right back up and keep fighting. Without question, it is a formidable foe.

Early in my therapy, I typically ask my patients how OCD interferes with their day-to-day life. Does it impact work, school, relationships, and pleasurable activities? For someone with OCD, the answer is usually yes. It doesn't have to be this way. Many people with OCD reclaim their lives and get to the point where the disorder is little more than an occasional nuisance. You may be feeling a bit overwhelmed right now, but that's perfectly normal. Please, keep reading. The focus going forward will be on developing a treatment plan that works for you.

Next Steps

Soon, we will get to work. But before we do so, let's cover a few important guidelines. Living with OCD is a 24/7 experience. It doesn't take any breaks, and so neither should the treatment. If you want to see significant progress, you should be doing exposure therapy work on it daily. If you take a break from it for even a week or so, the OCD will find ways to negate whatever progress you've made. Plus, when you successfully complete an exposure exercise and move on to another issue, you still need to pay attention to the ones you've already worked on. Make time to revisit older exposure exercises to ensure that you maintain progress.

Think of it as building your ERP muscles. They will get strong if you're consistent with your exercises but may atrophy if you're not. Also, as you go through this workbook, please do so at a pace that will maximize its effectiveness. If something doesn't seem clear, read it through until it does. The same is true before you engage in any of the exercises. It's crucial that you thoroughly understand them before you begin whatever exposure work you choose.

Lastly, be mindful of the concept "two steps forward, one step back." It most certainly applies to OCD therapy. Setbacks are a natural part of the process. They'll occur, and you'll feel frustrated when they do. As much as I would like to say otherwise, I would be misleading you if I were to convey that people get better and then rarely experience problems afterward.

Take, for example, this well-known quote from famed basketball player Michael Jordan: "I've missed more than 9,000 shots in my career. I've lost almost 300 games. Twenty-six times, I've been trusted to take the game winning shot and missed. I've failed over and over and over again in my life. And that is why I succeed."

Unlike Jordan, you probably won't have thousands of missteps as you tackle your OCD, nor should you think of ERP struggles as failures. The sentiment of the quote, however, is relevant. Allow yourself to accept the setbacks as the expected norms of the process. Keep your eye on the prize, which is to free yourself from the torment of OCD. It can be a fiendish problem. Just when you think you might have control over it, some other obsession gets thrown into the mix. It doesn't let go easily. You have to be more persistent than it is.

Wrap-Up

In this chapter, we took a deeper look at what lies ahead in this book: what to do about OCD. Much of the discussion so far has focused on ERP. This is a very specific form of CBT known to be the most effective treatment for OCD. As you've seen, exposure therapy can also be done through imagery. When done properly, it offers a very potent way to confront particularly troubling thoughts and images. Additionally, we've explored a little about mindfulness and ACT, as both have been shown to be useful strategies to augment ERP. I hope it's obvious at this point that OCD therapy is very different from traditional talk therapy. Sure, we do some talking in this therapy, but treating OCD is about developing a behavioral plan to ultimately weaken the disorder.

Before we dive into developing a treatment plan tailored to your OCD, I'd like you to consider the following questions:

What would you like to focus on first? I will show you how to decide on this a little later, but does anything stand out at this point to you?

___

___

___

How are you feeling at this point? Did some parts of this chapter scare you? Motivate you? I'm hoping it is more of the latter, but the former is to be expected.

What do you feel that you've learned in this chapter? Is anything confusing? Please make note of it. I'm hopeful it will be clarified as you read the next chapter.

In what ways do you think your OCD interferes in your life? Does it hinder work, school, relationships, fun activities? It's probably at least one, or maybe all. Please be specific as you list how OCD affects your life. It will be helpful to look back at this as we go through the process of working on the OCD. Being aware of these factors is a good way to assist you in staying motivated, especially as we tackle some of the more difficult obsessions and compulsions.

PART TWO

THE STEPS

STEP ONE

Get to the Heart of the Matter

AN IMPORTANT FIRST STEP in this process is to know what you're working on. I know, it sounds pretty obvious. I tell my clients that the more I know about their OCD, the better I can help them. This means spending a few days tracking all of their various obsessive thoughts and compulsive behaviors. For some this comes quickly, as their OCD may focus on just one form. For others it may take longer, as they struggle with various manifestations of it. For example, your OCD may be about checking compulsions, but someone else may have those plus compulsive counting and harm obsessions. Keep track of all of your compulsions. Consider sharing your list with others who are closest to you, as they may have some worthwhile observations. I've met with many people over the years who knew they had OCD but didn't think that some of their fears and behaviors were part of the disorder until they completed this task. This may be especially true with the lesser-known forms, such as existential OCD and relationship OCD.

Your Tracking Results

The easiest way to keep track of your OCD is to write down all of your obsessions and compulsions. You can use the space below if you like. If you have fears associated with putting thoughts down on paper or in some written form, make audio recordings of your obsessions or compulsions. Dictating into the notes app on your smartphone can be a great way to do this. Better yet, you could ask a friend or family member to write them down for you. It doesn't really matter to me how someone goes about doing this, but it is important that it gets done.

Once you've made your list, it's time to put it in hierarchal form. Typically, focus on obsessions and compulsions that are easier to work on first, then move on to the more difficult items. An important early step in this process is to start thinking about how strong your anxiety/discomfort level would be if you didn't complete a compulsion. For example, let's say you constantly check the stove top burners. How difficult would it be to turn them on, then turn them off one time, without checking to see if they're off? Many therapists use a tool called the SUDS scale, short for subjective units of distress scale (Wolpe, 1973), to determine anxiety levels when not performing specific compulsions. This can be done by thinking of numbers between 1 and 10 or 1 and 100. I prefer 1 and 100, since it allows for more specificity. A score of 1 is a state of calmness, and 100 is severe anxiety. For the latter, think panic attack or close to it.

OCD Fear Thermometer

Another good way of tracking anxiety levels is to look at some of the many OCD anxiety or fear "thermometers" or scales that are online. They follow a similar system to the SUDS scale. Here's an example:

91 to 100	*I feel as if I can't take this anymore. Panic-level anxiety.*
81 to 90	*Very uncomfortable. Unsure I can tolerate much more.*
71 to 80	*This is getting pretty tough. I'm hanging in there, but it's getting hard.*
61 to 70	*Definitely feeling uncomfortable, but still managing okay.*
51 to 60	*I don't really like this, but I can deal with it.*
41 to 50	*Moderate discomfort. Feeling the anxiety beginning to rise more.*
31 to 40	*Noticeable discomfort, but I can deal with it.*
21 to 30	*First real sign of anxiety. I don't really like it, but it's not much of a problem.*
11 to 20	*I feel a little uncomfortable, but I can ignore it.*
1 to 10	*Okay so far. Maybe just a passing twinge of unease.*

Results of Patrick's Tracking

Patrick is a former patient of mine. He had various fears associated with using most appliances at home. The primary fear was that if he didn't thoroughly check on an appliance, it could be left on and start a fire. It would be bad if his apartment caught on fire, but Patrick was more concerned about the fate of his cats and his neighbors. While each feared item was difficult to confront, he realized that some were more difficult than others. Here is what Patrick put together after our first session. The accompanying numbers are Patrick's estimate of how difficult each item might be to work on with using the 1 to 100 SUDS scale and referring to the OCD fear thermometer. I've noted the corresponding compulsion that would need to be resisted in parentheses below.

- Stove top burners (counting to four as he checked each burner) - 92
- Microwave oven (setting the time for 10 seconds and waiting for the beep) - 65
- The oven itself (opening and closing it multiple times while sticking his arm in to feel any heat) - 50

- TVs (each TV had to be turned to channel four before being turned off) - 34
- Computer (after shutting down he would keep his hand on top of his laptop until the warmth dissipated) - 45
- Coffee maker (unplugged it after each use) - 95
- Lights (switch had to be firmly in the down position and redone if he felt it wasn't) - 28
- Toaster oven (used only if he knew he was staying home for the remainder of the day) - 80
- Vacuum cleaner (left out in hallway for one full day until put back in closet) - 48
- Washing machine (never used hot setting) - 25

As I reviewed Patrick's list, I noticed something interesting that is often a part of someone's OCD: Sometimes the compulsions seemed related to the fear and sometimes they didn't. Take, for example, his coffee pot ritual. If it wasn't plugged in, he eliminated the possibility of some electrical malfunction causing a fire. On the other hand, Patrick's need to count to four as he checked each burner showed no connection to a potential fire. This reminds me of something I say probably every time I'm with my clients: "It's not our job to figure it out. We're just trying to get rid of as much of it as possible." Patrick understood that his behaviors didn't make much sense, but knowing that didn't stop him from feeling the need to perform them.

I suggest you avoid spending too much time figuring out the logic behind your obsessions and compulsions. Sure, facts can be useful. But be careful about how much research you do on your fears. Searching online can sometimes serve only to further scare you. You're better off asking someone you think might have the answer. But also be aware that it could evolve into reassurance seeking if you are asking the same questions over and over again because you're not feeling satisfied with the answers.

In my experience, OCD doesn't know much about logic. How likely is it for the washing machine to catch fire if hot water is used? I think most people would agree that the hot setting wouldn't exist if the risk of fire was strong. But many people I've treated will dismiss that kind of factual information and insist that just because something hasn't happened yet doesn't mean it won't. OCD has the power to overwhelm logic and have you think that there's always a first time.

Patrick's Fear of Fire Hierarchy

Patrick brought in his list of feared items to our second meeting. As we discussed his comfort level in resisting his various compulsions, we came up with the rankings together—as I mentioned earlier, this was a team approach. Here's what Patrick and I came up with for his first hierarchy, listing them in order of what might be easiest to work on first:

1. Use the washing machine with the water temperature set to hot. Do this without periodically checking to see if the machine is getting too warm or any other indicators to him that a fire could start.
2. Turn off the light switches quickly and with a gentle touch. Walk away without looking back at them.
3. Turn off each TV while it is on a random channel, just not on channel four.
4. Turn off the computer and walk away from it. Don't feel it for warmth.
5. Use the vacuum cleaner for at least five minutes, then place it directly in the closet. Do so without carefully checking that it doesn't touch anything else.
6. Cook something in the oven. Turn it off without putting his arms into the oven periodically to check the warmth.
7. Cook something in the microwave. After taking out the item, close the door and don't reset the microwave for 10 seconds to check that the appliance is actually off. Also, walk away from the kitchen to avoid any visual checking.
8. Make toast in the toaster oven. Turn it off once, and leave the apartment within the hour without checking to make sure the oven is off.
9. Boil some water with a stove top burner. Turn off the burner just one time, and without counting to four.
10. Make coffee in the coffee maker. Once it's done, walk away from the kitchen, leaving the coffee maker plugged in. It should also be kept plugged in when leaving the apartment later.

ADJUSTING THE HIERARCHY

A little later we will review how to actually do the ERP work with hierarchies. In the meantime, be aware that as you go through your hierarchies you'll need to adjust them. You really don't know how difficult it may be to work on any one item. You may reach an item on the hierarchy and realize that it's too challenging to take on—at least for now. If that happens, find an interim step to work on.

In Patrick's case, we came across this when working with his most challenging obsession, the coffee maker. Initially, the thought of leaving the coffee maker plugged in and leaving his apartment caused too much anxiety, so we broke it down into time segments. At first he left it plugged in and left for a few minutes to get his mail. Once he felt he mastered that, Patrick felt comfortable enough to go for a 15-minute walk. After that, he went out shopping for a few hours. Ultimately, he was able to go away for an entire weekend while leaving the coffee maker plugged in. Patrick's experience is very common. This is a reminder to not get down on yourself if you feel unable to work on something listed in your hierarchy. It simply means that you need to adjust the hierarchy into more manageable steps.

Other Sample Hierarchies

Let's take a look at some more hierarchies. No one could possibly list all possible hierarchies, since OCD is very creative and constantly coming up with new variations. What you'll see below are examples for some of the more common forms of OCD.

Contamination Fears

Michelle had a fear of germs. Wherever she went, she felt bombarded by fears of getting sick and ultimately dying. She was also terrified of getting other people sick, especially her young children. This took over her life. There were many places she and her family couldn't go. Michelle often prevented her children from visiting friends because of the fear that they'd pick up some illness. This is what eventually brought her to therapy: the recognition that her obsessive fears weren't interfering with just her life but also her children's lives. In our second meeting, Michelle came to the session with her tracking list, which led us to put together this hierarchy:

1. While driving her car, do so without wearing gloves.
2. When picking up her kids at school, walk to their classrooms without wearing gloves. Touch the doorknobs, backpacks, books, and other items that may have been in the classroom.
3. When putting her kids in the car, don't use hand sanitizer.
4. Don't wash her clothes or her children's clothes when they return home from school. She and the children would wear the clothes they wore to school for the rest of the day.
5. Go to the grocery store and use the cart without cleaning the handles and without wearing gloves.
6. When at the grocery store, select the cans and boxes that are first noticed, not the items she thinks were less likely touched.
7. Once home, no scrubbing fruits and vegetables with soap prior to putting them into the refrigerator.
8. Go to the mall without wearing gloves, and make sure to touch at least 10 items during her visit without cleaning her hands.
9. When in the mall, talk to a sales clerk and shake that person's hand when the conversation is finished—no handwashing or use of hand sanitizer afterward.
10. Allow her children to go over to a friend's home. When they return home, don't change their clothes.

"Hit-and-Run" OCD

Michael loved cars, especially sports cars. His prized possession was a classic 1965 Mustang convertible. He kept that car in mint condition, and anyone who knew Michael knew he loved that car. When we first started meeting, Michael told me he hadn't driven the car for about five years. He was worried about hitting someone. Even though he had never hit someone before, Michael was sure it was just a matter of time. He began taking public transportation everywhere, which wasn't always practical for him. Silicon Valley isn't like New York City or Chicago. Living there without a car makes it difficult to get places and to get there on time. Of course, ride-sharing services made this a little easier for him. But Michael still missed being able to drive his "baby," as he often called his Mustang.

COPING WITH UNCERTAINTY

We all live with uncertainty. It's part of life. We can't be 100 percent certain that we're never going to get sick by touching doorknobs with our bare hands. We aren't certain we'll never hit someone with our car or cause a fire by leaving a burner turned on. When we leave in the morning for work or school, how can we be sure that we, or our loved ones, will ever return? We can't. But most of us don't even think much about the uncertainty of life and go on each day.

However, people with OCD pursue certainty and are usually frustrated in that quest. An important component in living with OCD means living with the knowledge that sometimes bad things do happen. What I say to my clients is that their obsessive fear is so unlikely to occur, it doesn't warrant the attention they give it. The goal is to accept that bad things do happen, but not as frequently as someone with OCD believes that they do. Michelle, who struggled with contamination fears, needed to learn how to accept living with uncertainty. Her difficulty with doing so prior to therapy was disrupting the lives of her entire family and created an unrealistic expectation that she should be able to control bad things from happening.

The first step of treatment for Michael to start driving again was to create a hierarchy. Here's what we put together:

1. Get in the Mustang and pull it out of the driveway then back into the garage.
2. Take the car out for a drive around the block with his wife in the passenger seat. Don't ask her if he has hit someone with the car or even if he is getting too close to someone.
3. Do the same as number two, but this time go a few miles from home.
4. Drive alone this time, and pull the car onto the street and back into the garage.
5. Drive around the block with only what would be considered normal checking of the rearview and side mirrors. Do not get out of the car to check if anyone has been hit, and don't drive around the block for the same reason.
6. Drive about five miles away from home on a weekend afternoon.
7. Drive about five miles away from home during commute hours.

8. Drive near the local elementary school during off hours, but when some children are likely playing in the playground.
9. Drive to the same school just as school is getting out.
10. Drive to a local shopping mall on a weekend when there is likely to be plenty of people.

An important aspect to consider with Michael's hierarchy is the importance of avoiding any of the usual checking behaviors during any of the exercises on the hierarchy. This meant using mirrors normally, not driving especially slowly when passing cyclists, keeping a normal distance between his car and the cars in front of him, and not avoiding routes he knew would be busy with traffic.

Emotional Contamination

Sarah was a senior in high school when she developed the fear that she would do poorly in school if she sat too close to someone who was underperforming. This type of OCD, known as emotional contamination, is a term that many people don't recognize, including Sarah and her family at first. When they sought my help, I explained that this subtype of OCD described her fears of being associated with people that she didn't want to become like. Similarly, Sarah tried to avoid contact with people who appeared to be out of shape, those who lived in less well-to-do communities, people who abused drugs or alcohol, and homeless people. This severely disrupted Sarah's school life and her socialization; she felt compelled to avoid anyone who appeared to have such qualities, at least in her mind.

As Sarah and I worked on her hierarchy, this is what we developed:

1. Watch YouTube videos about homelessness.
2. Watch YouTube videos about homelessness and at the same time think that it's going to happen to her.
3. While at school, say hi to one of the girls she has been avoiding. This girl and Sarah were once close, but that changed as Sarah's OCD worsened.
4. Walk past a boy at school whom Sarah knows smokes marijuana.
5. Sit with friends during lunch and don't change seats when someone she worries about joins them.
6. When returning home from school, wear the same clothes she had on while she was there.
7. Walk downtown and pass by a homeless person without crossing the street.

8. Hand a dollar bill to a homeless person.
9. Say hi to someone at school with whom she had been friends and who had recently returned from being in juvenile hall.
10. Talk to a family friend who dropped out of high school and is currently unemployed.

Like any exposure hierarchy, we set some guidelines for the compulsive actions she needed to resist. This included not washing her hands, using hand sanitizer, or taking a shower after doing the exposures. It was also important that her family members not participate in these rituals, either. Prior to starting her therapy, Sarah would insist that her family engage in the same cleaning compulsions she did. Once Sarah's parents understood that doing so was actually contributing to the OCD, those types of behaviors stopped.

Harm Obsessions

Catherine might be the kindest person I've ever met. The phrase "wouldn't hurt a fly" describes her perfectly. Early in her therapy, I would often hear Catherine say that she'd harm herself before harming anyone else. Of course, OCD often targets whatever someone holds most dear. In Catherine's case, the disorder focused on her harming others. She avoided knives, watching TV shows with any violence, or reading newspapers entirely. When reading, words such as *kill*, *murder*, and *death* would trigger the compulsion of repeating the same words and placing the word *not* in front of them. Here is the hierarchy we developed:

1. Watch the news on TV and don't put the TV on mute once a story with violence comes on.
2. Write the words *kill*, *murder*, and *death* on a piece of paper and leave the paper where she would see it frequently throughout the day.
3. Look at knives on the internet for five minutes at a time.
4. Look at knives on the internet for five minutes while also thinking to herself that she could lose control and stab someone.
5. At home, take a steak knife and put it where she can see it while watching TV.
6. At home, take a steak knife and hold on to it while watching TV.
7. At home, take a steak knife and hold on to it while watching TV with family members.
8. At home, take a steak knife and hold on to it while watching TV with family members and purposely think about stabbing them.

9. Read a story in the news about a murder and insert her name each time the name of the perpetrator is used.
10. Write out a story about her losing control, stabbing someone, and eventually having to spend the rest of her life in jail.

As Catherine did her exposure work, we learned that she had some rituals that weren't apparent while we developed the hierarchy. These included her praying during exposures or saying to herself "just kidding" when the exposures required her to say or think about causing harm to someone. I explained that these acts would ultimately defeat the exposure work. In short, she needed to avoid these rituals while she conducted her exposure work. If not, she wouldn't be able to reach a point of what's called habituation—where there is no longer distress and anxiety associated with these thoughts. It's a critical concept in working with OCD and one that even the most minor of compulsive acts may disrupt. If you're going to do ERP, you've got to be all in. Catherine understood this and quickly saw some relief as she did her exposures and at the same time eliminated any compulsions.

Symmetry and Orderliness

Jonathan was 40 years old when he started therapy. He was married and had two daughters, ages 10 and 5. He'd had OCD since childhood but never before sought treatment. He had heard about exposure therapy but was frightened by it. He began to consider it only with the encouragement of his wife.

Jonathan's OCD was worsening over time. It contributed to his being late to meetings at work, which resulted in him being put on a performance plan. Earlier, his fears had focused on doing poorly at school or something bad happening to him. But after he got married, they focused on something bad happening to his wife, and later he became concerned about their children. To ward off these fears, Jonathan would arrange household items in certain orders, including bottles in the refrigerator, kitchen utensils, and pens and pencils. Here is the hierarchy we developed for him:

1. Turn the ketchup bottle so its label is pointed toward the inside of the refrigerator and all other labels are pointed out.
2. Take several other items in the refrigerator and do the same thing. This time purposely think of something bad happening to him. Nothing specific—just a vague thought that something bad may happen.
3. Rearrange books in the bookshelf so that they are no longer all the same distance from the back of the shelf.

4. Take some socks and put them in the underwear drawer and take some underwear and put them in the socks drawer.
5. Purposely move a picture on the wall so that it is tilted slightly to one side.
6. Do the same with pictures on countertops.
7. Take several files at home and place them out of order in the filing cabinet.
8. Move all of his pens in a jar so that they are pointed in different directions. While doing this, think of him and his family getting into a car accident.
9. Do the same with silverware in the drawer, this time thinking of a family member dying.
10. Reset the digital clocks at home so that they are all at different times. They need to be different by only seconds, but they must be different. While doing this, think of him and his family dying in a plane crash.

THOUGHT-ACTION FUSION

The essence of thought-action fusion is when someone has a harmful thought of some kind and believes that it's the same as having done the act or evidence that the thought will turn into reality, according to a 2007 study published in *Advances in Psychiatric Treatment*. An example is when a person with obsessive thoughts about losing control and stabbing a family member believes that the thought itself is proof that it's going to occur. Of course, having a thought is very different from actually doing it. As one of my clients recently said to me, if we arrested people for having bad thoughts, our jails would be overflowing.

But thought-action fusion is very real for people with OCD. Anywhere from 80 to 90 percent of people without OCD have the same intrusive thoughts and images, according to a 2005 study published in *Theory, Research, and Treatment*. The difference is that someone without OCD dismisses the thoughts as nonsensical mental chatter. A person with OCD becomes frightened by the possibilities of their intrusive thoughts. While this is sometimes reassuring to people with OCD, it generally doesn't stop the obsessive worry. OCD is smarter than that. Sooner or later, most people with this form of OCD will resume wondering if they're the exception and end up performing their compulsive rituals. Once again, this speaks to the importance of exposure therapy. The proof is in the doing.

Keep in mind that I wasn't asking Jonathan to think anything new. He'd already had these kinds of thoughts. The difference here is to have him indulge those thoughts without engaging in his compulsive actions. Sure, these are awful thoughts, but once he began having them on purpose they started to lose their meaning.

Putting Together Hierarchies

Now that you have seen the OCD fear thermometer and reviewed the hierarchies put together by some of my clients with OCD, it's time to begin working on your own action plan. You've already put together a list of obsessive thoughts and compulsive behaviors. Now we're going to put it together in hierarchal fashion. Be sure to list them from easiest to hardest. Also, you want to have a separate hierarchy for each form of OCD you're going to work on. If this doesn't quite make sense to you, please go back and review sections before proceeding with your hierarchy.

STEP TWO

Applying Cognitive Therapy Techniques

AS WAS DISCUSSED EARLIER, treating OCD is primarily about doing exposure therapy. The focus of cognitive therapy, however, is on identifying faulty thought patterns, and with OCD there is no shortage of those. In this chapter we will concentrate on some cognitive therapy strategies that will enhance the process of the exposure work.

This was a recent conversation between me and a client, regarding his fears about being sent to an alternate universe if he didn't perform his compulsions properly. The idea behind the conversation is to identify his thought patterns so we could develop a meaningful and effective exposure therapy plan. I would consider this to be an example of existential OCD.

Client:	*If I don't walk back to that spot with the crack in it, I'm going to be sent to a different dimension.*
Me:	*Is there evidence that supports that belief? Can you tell me about it?*
Client:	*I watched a movie where something similar to that happened to someone.*
Me:	*Besides the movie, have you ever heard of that happening?*
Client:	*No. I don't think so.*
Me:	*So your fear stems from having seen a movie?*
Client:	*Yes. It would seem so. But how do you know it couldn't happen?*
Me:	*I don't know, but I've never heard of it. It seems very unlikely to me. Do you know of anyone else who is worrying about this?*
Client:	*No.*
Me:	*Can we agree that your fears are based on some assumptions you're making?*
Client:	*Yes. I guess so.*

This brief discussion helped the client see that his fears were based on assumptions he made from watching a science fiction movie. He understood that no hard evidence supported his beliefs, though it still didn't stop him from performing his compulsions. Our cognitive therapy-based discussions helped him become more willing to try his exposure therapy exercises, which he conducted with great success.

Identifying Negative Thoughts

We all have negative thoughts multiple times per day. Mostly, they come and go without much attention. Problems develop when these thoughts start to get stuck and cause significant distress. An important first step in doing cognitive therapy is identifying the negative thoughts themselves. Learning how to think differently about them comes later.

WHAT'S THE DIFFERENCE BETWEEN COGNITIVE THERAPY AND PROVIDING REASSURANCE?

The essence of cognitive therapy is learning to think from a more rational perspective. The goal is to find new ways of thinking that make sense, which can help you move away from feelings of distress. In cognitive therapy, it's believed that our faulty thought patterns set the stage for distress and that thinking more logically can free us from that cycle. This shouldn't be confused with positive thinking. In cognitive therapy, the goal is to look for reasons to support new perspectives, not simply telling yourself that you have nothing to worry about.

In my practice I prefer to engage in limited discussions about obsessive fears and spend more time looking for alternate ways of thinking about the fears. If someone can recognize that they've driven 1,000 times without ever hitting a pedestrian, those numbers may help them think more rationally about the safety of driving. The same is true for many other obsessive thoughts. Take a very common fear associated with OCD: someone dying from touching the handles of shopping carts. I haven't researched that specific subject but feel confidently that millions of people safely use shopping carts each year without being rushed to emergency rooms.

Seeking reassurance, however, is different. It is the repeated asking of a specific question after already having been given the answer. The example of the shopping cart is appropriate here. A cognitive approach could involve asking the person to identify the evidence that supports such a belief. That would likely lead to the realization that the evidence is simply based on the person's assumptions rather than on any factual information. The person may briefly be satisfied with that, but fast-forward a minute, an hour, or a day later, and that person may be back with either the very same question or some variation of it. What started out as a useful cognitive therapy exercise on the dangers of touching shopping cart handles has suddenly changed. When it appears that these cognitive therapy-based discussions have turned into reassurance seeking, I make it a point to identify that to my clients and no longer answer those questions.

Here's an example of my own: Several years ago, I was asked to meet with a hospital administrator who was interested in developing an OCD program. I said I was happy to do so but needed to leave no later than 3:00 p.m. The meeting was going well; the discussion was engaging, with lots of questions. Then, promptly at 3:00 p.m., the administrator wrapped up the meeting. I thought, *Wow, what happened there? I thought this was going pretty well.*

I struggled to figure out why the meeting abruptly ended. I was confused until I asked the important cognitive therapy question: What else could explain what just happened? That was when I realized I had mentioned at the beginning of the meeting that I needed to leave no later than 3:00 p.m. Was it possible that the way the meeting ended had little to do with my performance and everything to do with the time constraints? Probably so. My distress over this meeting was rooted in my own distorted thought process, not the reality of the situation. I suddenly felt a whole lot better.

Negative Thoughts: An Example

You've already identified some negative thoughts based on the tracking you did about your obsessions. Let's see if we can work on those thoughts with cognitive therapy. The primary tool used in cognitive therapy is the automatic thought record. Essentially, this calls for keeping track of your negative thoughts while developing skills to think from a more rational perspective. Here's a sample automatic thought record for someone with harm obsessions pertaining to losing control and stabbing a family member:

Date/time: Saturday, 9:30 p.m.

Situation: Watching TV with my parents.

Automatic thought: I'm going to grab that knife away from my mother and stab both her and my father.

How much do you believe the thought? 90 percent.

Evidence that the thought is TRUE: I see the knife, and I'm having terrible thoughts of stabbing them. I have a strong urge to actually do it this time.

Evidence that the thought may not be TRUE: These thoughts have happened before, and I've never done anything. I've never actually picked up a knife when I've felt this way.

More rational thought: This is my OCD acting up again. These thoughts are scary, but I know they will pass as they always do. This is another example of thought-action fusion. It doesn't mean I'm going to do anything. They're just thoughts.

How much do you believe the thought now? 40 percent.

Negative Thoughts: Let's Try One More

This next automatic thought record pertains to someone who has obsessions associated with becoming a child molester. For obvious reasons, this tends to be one of the more disturbing obsessions for someone with OCD. It may be comforting for people who experience this to know that this form of OCD is actually quite common.

Date/time: Sunday, 3:00 p.m.

Situation: Taking my daughter to the playground.

Automatic thought: That girl my daughter is playing with is very pretty. Why am I having that kind of thought about an eight-year-old? Do I find her sexually attractive?

How much do you believe the thought? 75 percent.

Evidence that the thought is TRUE: Why else would I be having these thoughts if I didn't want to have sex with her? Normal people don't have these thoughts.

Evidence that the thought may not be TRUE: These thoughts upset me. If I really wanted to have sex with her, I would find these thoughts pleasurable.

More rational thought: It's normal to have these types of thoughts. I really don't believe that I want to do anything. I don't like them, but they've happened before and have gone away before. This is another OCD episode I have to deal with.

How much do you believe the thought now? 30 percent.

EXERCISE: THOUGHT RECORDS

Like most things in life, learning how to use the automatic thought record takes practice. Over time the process will happen more quickly, and your ability to talk back to the obsessive thoughts will come more naturally. You may even get to a point where you don't need to write it all down.

Date/time: ______________________________

Situation: ______________________________

Automatic thought: ______________________________

Evidence that the thought is TRUE: ______________________________

____

Evidence that the thought may not be TRUE: ______________________________

____

More rational thought: ______________________________

How much do you believe the thought now? ______________________________

Cognitive Distortions

Cognitive distortions are basically faulty patterns of thinking—again, something in which we all engage. Being diligent about using the automatic thought record allows for recognizing these distortions and developing the capacity to think from a more rational perspective. When you recognize you've fallen into these patterns, then learn to think from a new perspective, that's when you gain the power to transform. As many as 20 cognitive distortions have been identified; below is a list of those that I encounter the most when working with OCD.

Catastrophizing

This is quite likely the cognitive distortion that I encounter most when treating OCD. Think of it as playing out the worst-case scenario in your mind. For example, it's not enough that you're convinced there's going to be a fire if you leave the coffee pot on; your house is going to burn down and take the rest of the neighborhood with it. You may survive this horrible chain of events, but you'll spend the rest of your life in jail for not taking the necessary precautions to prevent it.

Jumping to Conclusions

This distortion is generally divided into two types. First is mind reading, when you believe you know what other people are thinking without sufficient evidence to support those thoughts. My meeting with the hospital administrator is a perfect example. The second is fortune-telling, where you already know that something will turn out badly. How many people with OCD *don't* engage in this one?

Overgeneralization

One bad thing happening doesn't make it a pattern. Someone with OCD, however, may hear a story about a pedestrian being hit with a car, then assume it is inevitable that he or she will hit someone as well.

Emotional Reasoning

You assume your feelings are an indication of the way things must be. In other words, if you feel scared of getting sick because you've touched a menu in a restaurant, then there must be some truth to your thoughts.

Personalization

You see yourself as responsible for something without any real evidence to support that belief. An example would be walking past a nail on a street and later hearing that someone got into an accident because of having had a flat tire on the freeway. You may believe that it was your fault for not picking up the nail.

Black-and-White or All-or-Nothing Thinking

Something terrible is either going to happen or it isn't. There's no in-between. If there's a car accident, everyone will die from it. If the front door isn't locked, something will be stolen, and the dogs will get out and get killed in the process. The idea that the door could be left open and nothing would happen isn't even considered.

Mental Filtering

This is essentially ignoring the positive aspects of something and instead focusing on the negatives. A student with OCD may earn mostly As in high school but instead focus on the one B grade and how that may negatively influence their future.

"Should" Statements

This essentially drives scrupulosity, which is best defined as an obsession driven by unrealistically harsh moral or ethical standards. An example might be inadvertently losing a gum wrapper, berating yourself for doing something wrong, and ultimately believing that you will get into trouble for littering.

Magical Thinking

I see this a lot with counting compulsions and other behaviors. An example would be walking through a doorway 10 times without having a bad thought because if you don't, that "just right" feeling will never come. Another could be needing to have the TV volume on level five or you won't get into your college of choice.

Thought-Action Fusion

Having a bad thought is essentially the same as having done the terrible act, or the thought itself may serve as proof that the action may have occurred. This is common in scrupulosity, as someone may believe that they are morally bad for even having had a negative thought about another person.

Which cognitive distortions do you identify with the most?

___

___

___

Now it's your turn. I'm sure some of these cognitive distortions resonate with you. Which ones stand out? How about writing some examples of those with which you identify?

___

___

___

___

Core Beliefs

Just like we all have automatic thoughts, everyone has core beliefs. Your core beliefs are deeply held views that usually stem from early childhood experiences. Hopefully, they're positive ones associated with how we generally view ourselves and the world around us. In OCD, however, negative thoughts surface and will dictate how we often respond to certain situations.

If you've struggled with OCD for years, it can also shape these beliefs. Examples of common core beliefs influenced by your OCD can include "I'm unlovable," "I'm a bad person," "I'm dangerous," "I'm untrustworthy," "I'm vulnerable," "I have to be perfect," "I have to be in control," "The world is dangerous," and "People can't be trusted." Your automatic thoughts tend to stem from these beliefs, and so learning how to reshape them is critically important.

Of course, we can't change our core beliefs unless we know what they are. One way to identify core beliefs is the "downward arrow technique" devised by Dennis

Greenberger and Christine A. Padesky in their book, *Mind Over Mood: Change How You Feel by Changing the Way You Think*. The technique involves a series of questions to identify core beliefs. Here are two examples of using this technique.

Downward Arrow Example 1

Let's get back to Catherine. She's my client with a harm obsession.

Automatic thought:	*"I keep having this urge to stab someone."*
↓	*(What does that say about me?)*
	"That I can't be left alone with knives."
	(If that's true, what does that say about me?)
	"People shouldn't risk being near me."
	(And if that's true, what does that mean about me?)
Core belief:	*"I'm a dangerous person."*

Downward Arrow Example 2

Up next is Peter, who has scrupulosity and is often tormented by blasphemous thoughts against God and his religion.

Automatic thought:	*"I have bad thoughts about God in church."*
↓	*(What does that say about me?)*
	"I'm not faithful to God."
	(If that's true, what does that mean for me?)
	"I will go to hell."
	(If that's true, what does that say about me?)
Core belief:	*"I'm a bad person."*

Changing Core Beliefs

Our core beliefs are so deeply held, which makes them quite a challenge to change. Changing them can be done, however, using ERP. The exposure experiments will help you reshape your thought patterns. This will become clearer as we dig into that therapy a little later in the workbook.

Another useful strategy is to look for evidence that doesn't support the core beliefs that cause you to have detrimental thoughts about yourself. This technique can lead you to develop new beliefs that are healthier and more accurate representations of who you are, according to *Mind Over Mood*. As I did this with Catherine, she recalled that she liked volunteering for various organizations, which included recording books for the blind and handing out food to the homeless. Peter, on the other hand, talked about how people at church often turned to him for guidance and how important it is for him to give financial support to his many charities.

Throughout the process with both, neither could actually give any real examples of being bad or dangerous. The only "evidence" was the intrusive thoughts, which really is evidence only of them having OCD.

EXERCISE: THE DOWNWARD ARROW TECHNIQUE

Ordinarily, it should take only three or four questions to get to a core belief. As you've seen previously, these questions are typically along the lines of "What does that thought say about me?" and "If true, what would that mean about me?"

Automatic thought:

What does that thought mean about me?

And what would that mean about me?

And if true, what would that mean about me?

Core belief:

Additional Cognitive Strategies

I'm not convinced that cognitive therapy techniques alone are the best way to manage OCD. But I do believe some strategies are helpful and worth mentioning. These aren't meant as substitutes for ERP, but they certainly could make that process a little easier. If your obsessive beliefs weaken even a little after engaging in one of these techniques, you may be more willing to engage with the exposure work. Below are some additional cognitive therapy strategies I have found to have some benefit in working with people with OCD.

"This Is Just My OCD"

Sounds simple. For some people it's useful to identify certain thoughts as just part of their OCD. It can help create some distance between what you know to be true and the nonsense that the OCD is trying to get you to believe. Of course, this works only if you're willing to believe what you're trying to tell yourself. This is going to be especially difficult, however, for someone who has little insight or is fairly convinced of their beliefs.

"If You Had to Bet"

This is one of my favorite strategies. Most people with OCD know that their obsessional beliefs aren't true, or at least they are willing to consider the possibility. This approach forces you to make a decision by working to eliminate the quest for certainty. For example, let's say you're having trouble convincing yourself that the garage door is closed. You're likely to be thinking to yourself that you're pretty sure it's closed, but you're not fully convinced. What if you had to place some money on it? Is it open or closed? You can answer only yes or no—"maybe," "I'm not sure," or "I need to check" aren't options. This strategy is an attempt to get you to make a definitive choice.

I've found this technique to be very effective. Most people with OCD make the right choice. The challenge is to stick with your answer and not act on the compulsion. This is very similar to the "wise mind" concept in dialectical behavior therapy (DBT) from Marsha Linehan's *Skills Training Manual for Treating Borderline Personality Disorder*. Linehan calls for you to trust what you believe and really know to be right. Of course, with OCD that's often easier said than done.

How Would Someone You Know Answer That?

Most people with OCD have someone in their life who doesn't have OCD. It can be helpful to think about how that person might react to a particular OCD challenge you're facing. If you touched something you think might be contaminated and feel the need to take a shower, think about if the person who doesn't have OCD would do the same. If the answer is no and that person is someone you trust, it may influence your line of thinking. This is different from asking for reassurance, which is when you ask someone else for information about your obsession. As we discussed earlier, that is not a recommended strategy. However, if thinking that other people wouldn't worry like you is helpful, there is some obvious value in that.

Is There Scientific Evidence Supporting This Belief?

Do you wash your hands 10 times a day and spend 20 minutes doing it each time? Is there scientific evidence you can point to that supports this behavior as necessary to fight off illness? It is unlikely. This line of thinking can help you understand that your actions are based on your assumptions rather than fact.

Use Past Experience as a Gauge to Assess for the Likelihood of Danger

This is an excellent technique for people with driving obsessions. Assuming you're still driving, how many times have you been behind the wheel this past week? Maybe 10 times? How many times have you hit someone? What about in the past month? How many times have you hit someone? Let's take it out even further. How often did you drive in the past year? Anywhere between 500 and 1,000 times. So, how many times have you hit someone with your car?

Whenever I ask a client these questions, the answer has always been "zero." Always. Now, it is possible to hit someone with your car, but the likelihood isn't very high. This strategy allows for a more realistic assessment of risk. For some people with OCD, it can be very effective; however, still some hold on to the belief that "there's always a first time."

The "Rules" of OCD

As debilitating as OCD can be, many people who have it do find ways to function in the world. Oftentimes, this means developing your own set of rules so that you can compartmentalize and get on with life. This allows you to temporarily overlook some of your obsessions and resist some compulsive behaviors when you wouldn't otherwise be able to do so. The rules that you've designed may not make sense to anyone else, but they do to you. Here are a couple of examples from my practice.

Laura lived with her terrible fear of knives for most of her adult life. She used only the dullest of knives, and even those caused some worry. Her job, however, was at a printing company, and it involved using some very sharp items to cut paper products. One day in my office, she went through her purse, and she pulled out a box cutter, which is really nothing more than a razor blade. I looked at her in amazement and asked, "What are you doing carrying around a box cutter? I don't think there are many things that are sharper than that."

She laughed and told me that she had forgotten that she'd put it in her purse. Then she said, "Look, I have to work, and I need to use box cutters sometimes." Laura was able to compartmentalize her fear of knives so she could perform the duties required by her job. Many people with OCD are very good at using this coping mechanism. Essentially, if needed, they can suspend their obsessive worries and compulsive actions if the situations warrant it. I see this often if doing a compulsion would result in some embarrassment. However, there are many others with OCD who can't compartmentalize and will still engage in their compulsions regardless of the embarrassment or disruptions to life they may cause.

Stephanie presents us with another good example. She first showed signs of contamination fears as a teenager, but it exploded to a new level when her son was born. By the time he was five months, Stephanie was sterilizing all of the baby's clothes with very specific cleaning products, and the baby's father wasn't even allowed to touch his own son. This resulted in almost complete isolation.

My office was one of the few places she went, and even then she brought a blanket to sit on. One day she told me this story of changing the baby's diaper. Ordinarily, she would put the baby on a new towel, but this time she couldn't find any. Instead, she used a newspaper and placed her son directly on it. I was flabbergasted. I said to her, "I'm having trouble understanding this. You're terrified of anything that's not absolutely clean touching your baby, but you placed him on newspaper while changing his diaper?" She simply replied, "I couldn't find anything else." She allowed for this exception, which was a new rule she made for herself out of necessity, just as Laura did with the box cutter. Both stories are further evidence that it's not important to work out the logic associated with your obsessive thoughts. Attempting to make sense of them will only further frustrate you. The focus should remain on how to reduce their power over you and find ways to live with the disorder. Having said that, I do feel it is useful to know when you're making up rules in an effort to manage your OCD.

People with OCD are some of the most creative problem solvers I know. What about you? Are there any cognitive strategies you use for yourself and any rules you've established in trying to cope with OCD? If so, please write them down here. You, too, may find it helpful to identify that some of the rules you live by are based on your own set of assumptions rather than on facts.

Wrap-Up

We've covered quite a bit of information about cognitive therapy, including automatic thoughts, core beliefs, the automatic thought record, and the downward arrow technique. You may be feeling somewhat fatigued at this point—feel free to take a break. But before you do, please take a moment to write down any questions you may have, comments about what you've learned, and what you're hoping to work on next.

STEP THREE

Work with ERP

DANIELLE WAS IN HER MID-THIRTIES when she first came to see me. At home she engaged in a series of checking behaviors that she couldn't control. Everything that had some type of an on-off switch or a door/latch was checked: the stove, lights, TV, computer, car, garage door, front door, back door, washing machine, dryer, windows. Remarkably, like so many of my clients, she functioned at a very high level. She had a good job, was married, had a young daughter, and was very active socially. It just took her a long time to leave her home because of all this checking. Her obsessive fears were many: a break-in, a fire, her children getting hurt. She even worried that a burglar would get hurt entering her home, and all of it would be her fault. Her OCD fears and checking behaviors often made her late for work and social gatherings and contributed to considerable marital tension at times.

Danielle had spent eight years in prior therapy with several different therapists. They were all well meaning, but they didn't know how to treat OCD. They assumed these fears and behaviors had something to do with Danielle's childhood experiences and took her down the path of exploratory therapy in a quest to develop new insights into her obsessions and compulsions. While Danielle felt that some discussions were in fact quite interesting, the therapy didn't lessen her OCD. In fact, it seemed only to worsen over time.

I worked with Danielle first on helping her gain a better understanding of how OCD is treated and the rationale behind doing exposure therapy. As I find with many clients, she was in fact relieved to know that we wouldn't be digging into her family background much and would instead keep our attention on reducing her OCD symptoms as much as possible. She especially liked that the therapy would be skills based, as she would be learning the tools needed to more effectively cope with her various obsessions and compulsions.

Danielle found her ERP work with me to be an entirely different experience. During our time together, her obsessive worries weakened substantially as she disengaged from most of her compulsive behaviors. My hope as we go forward is that like Danielle, you, too, will be able to utilize the state-of-the-art ERP techniques that worked so well for her. While Danielle's OCD sometimes reemerges as occasional flare-ups, her life is no longer taken over by it. She has been late for work only once in the past six months, and that was the fault of a flat tire. In fact she told me that it was a relief to worry about something so normal instead of the obsessive thoughts that had plagued her for so much of her life.

As we work through this chapter, you will be faced with the challenge of doing ERP therapy, perhaps for the first time. You've already put together your hierarchies, and now it's time to begin the process of truly reclaiming your life from the grasp of OCD.

ERP Guidelines

As we explore ERP, it is important to consider some helpful guidelines for doing so. Please read these before engaging in your exposure exercises.

Find a Coach

A coach can be a family member or friend. The most important criterion is that the person be someone you trust and whom you believe is supportive of you. A coach isn't a therapist; it's someone who encourages you and reminds you to do the ERP, without giving any reassurance. Knowing what OCD is, how it affects you, and what to do and what not to do during exposure therapy are all important qualities in a coach.

Additionally, it is helpful to discuss what you need from your coach ahead of time. For example, if you say you're not ready to tackle a particular exposure item on your hierarchy, it's perfectly acceptable for your coach to push you a little by saying something, such as, "Do you think you can try?" If, however, your response to that is "No, I just can't do it yet," that has to be accepted. Pushing someone to go beyond what they're ready to do is not okay, whether it's coming from a therapist or a coach. Ultimately, you're the one in control of deciding what types of exposures you're going to do and for how long you're going to do them.

We could also just as easily use the term *cheerleader* instead of *coach*. Comments such as "You're doing great!," "I know it's tough, but do you think you can try to continue with the ERP?" and "Good job! That was a hard one!" are all very encouraging and demonstrate that the coach is providing the type of support that is needed. Conversely, comments such as "You know that can't hurt you" and "No one has ever died from that" are reassurance based and not helpful. Many people leave my office feeling newly motivated after a session to do their exposure therapy, but once home they have trouble maintaining consistency. It's understandable. OCD fights back and can cause tremendous anxiety. If this happens to you, a coach can help give you the encouragement you may need to keep the process going. In contrast, if this person gets angry with you, blames you, or makes you feel guilty, it's time for a new coach.

Consider Readjusting Your Hierarchy

As you work through your hierarchy, keep in mind something that was mentioned earlier: Most people get stuck at some point in the process. If you've reached an item on your hierarchy where it feels like the next step is too hard, try inserting an interim step. For example, if you find it too difficult to leave your home for an hour after turning off lights, try leaving for 30 minutes instead. When you're ready, you can bump up your away time to an hour. During an individual exposure exercise, try to stay with it until the anxiety drops to about half of what it was when you started. For example, if the SUDS level registered about 80 when you started a particular exposure, try to stay with the exercise until it reaches level 40. Another good rule of thumb is to wait until your anxiety comes down to a SUDS level of 20 before you move on to the next item.

You Maintain Control over the Exposure Experiments

Remember, no one will force you to do your exposure work. Yes, you'll need to push yourself to get better, but nothing good ever comes from being forced to do something that you're not ready to do. I recall a patient's husband once threw dirty clothes on her in an attempt to speed the process up. Clearly, he felt frustrated and later recognized that he had gone too far. The episode seemed only to heighten her obsessive worries and caused her to wonder how much she could really trust him. When my clients tell me that they're not feeling ready to work on something, I usually follow up with two questions: "Are you sure?" and "Do you feel you can try it?" If the answer is yes to the first and no to the second, I take it as a sign that we need to work on something else.

Avoid Asking or Being Given Reassurance

As I mentioned earlier, seeking reassurance is probably the most common of all compulsions. I do recognize that reassurance can sometimes provide momentary relief, but that's the point. It's only momentary. To truly get better means being able to learn for yourself what is worth worrying about and what isn't. If you rely on someone else doing this for you, it will disrupt your ability to do it for yourself.

Be Aware of Any Avoidance While Doing Exposure Therapy

Are you wiping your hands on your pants after doing an exposure exercise for contamination? Are you reading the news online to see if anyone in your neighborhood was hit by a car after you were out driving? If you've answered yes to those questions, you're not fully engaged in your ERP. As was noted earlier, it's not enough to expose yourself to a feared circumstance. You also need to not perform the corresponding compulsion. Equally important is not to conduct any mental compulsions during an exposure. For example, praying that you don't cause any harm during exposure therapy that involves knives is really just another compulsion and will interfere with what you're trying to accomplish.

Pushing Past Avoidance

I understand how tempting it is to avoid part of an exposure exercise. ERP is challenging, and, unfortunately, for it to be effective, it must be somewhat uncomfortable. If you're only halfway in, you won't get the intended relief. As one of my clients once said to me, think of it as "short-term pain for long-term gain."

Consider Using a Reward System

A reward system can be a great motivating tool. I remember once mentioning this concept to the parents of one of my clients. At the next session, they returned with a new car. I should've been clearer, because a new car for their child really wasn't the type of reward I had in mind. Going out for ice cream, to a movie, or for a walk on the beach was more of what I meant. Remember, the reward is for putting in the effort to do the ERP and not for succeeding with it. Again, this is hard work, but success will ultimately come when you put in the effort.

Use Imagery

Sometimes doing real-life exposure is too difficult at first. If that's the case, try doing some imaginal exposure. If you have emotional contamination, for example, you may first purposely think about becoming unintelligent or homeless. When the anxiety associated with that subsides, have some real contact with people who have the qualities you fear. There also may come a time when doing the imaginal exposure will be the first-line treatment of choice. We'll discuss imaginal exposure in the next chapter.

Be Consistent

Truly working on OCD means doing some exposure work every single day. OCD doesn't take a break from trying to cause you trouble, so you shouldn't take a break from tackling it. This isn't to say that you're expected to work on your OCD at all hours throughout the day. But make the commitment to work on your hierarchy. Set aside at least 30 minutes per day for some exposure work. If there are days where you just can't find the time, try to make those the exception rather than the rule. Get a calendar and plan out the days and times when you're going to do the exposure exercises. This may help you stay accountable to the process and avoid the dreaded P word—*procrastination*.

The *H* Word

How much did you enjoy homework in school? Most people would say they didn't like it at all, but as with school, it's a necessary part of the learning process. This is similar to what was described in the prior guideline about consistency. In this case, "homework" is the work you'll do with your coach or therapist. If you've agreed to do homework, make the effort to get it done. If you're doing exposure therapy only during your time with your therapist or coach, getting better becomes a much more difficult process. Remember, the goal is getting better, and getting better means working on the OCD frequently during the week.

Spontaneous Exposures

Gaining control over OCD is all about doing exposure therapy. We've discussed in great detail how to plan for it, but life often produces unexpected challenges. Let's say you're on a plane and you have contamination fears. The man sitting next to you occasionally bumps elbows with you, but not often enough for you to ask him to stop. What do you do? Do you pull out some hand wipes to clean your elbow each time he touches you (as some of my clients have)? Do you alert the flight attendant that the person next to you is brushing up against you every so often? Most likely not. It's not as if you can say to yourself, "Hey, I'm not working on this part of my hierarchy yet" and expect that the situation will suddenly change. If the situation presents itself, take it as an opportunity to do some unplanned exposure therapy. John Lennon famously said, "Life is what happens while you are busy making other plans." The same could be said for dealing with OCD—ERP is what happens while you're busy making other plans.

Be Willing to Take Risks

No one really likes doing exposure therapy. It's anxiety provoking, and it can be scary. But it works. If you have any questions about whether an exposure exercise is actually dangerous, be sure to ask your coach or someone else who doesn't have OCD—just be sure that it doesn't turn into you seeking reassurance. A simple comment about how an exposure exercise seems like a good idea is all that person needs to say. Please don't prod them for comments about danger or risk unless it's obviously something that comes with some element of real danger. More often, you'll know when an exposure exercise actually may be dangerous because you won't do it. I've never come across a situation when doing ERP meant putting a person in a situation of actual risk.

Having said all of that, please know that living a full life does come with risk. Most people who drive understand that there are thousands of traffic-related deaths each year, yet they still get into their cars every day. Who's to say you're not going to choke on some food when eating? It happens, and some people have died because of it. Is that reason to stop eating? No, of course not.

Be Proud of Yourself

The exposure exercises may not seem like a big deal to someone without OCD, but we know different. Embarking on this task takes a tremendous amount of courage and persistence. My OCD patients are some of the bravest people I know. Please never lose sight of that.

While I recognize that this next sentence probably isn't likely to dissuade your obsessive worry, it may provide some semblance of comfort: There are no known instances of someone with OCD actually doing the feared action, according to a 2009 article published in Advances in Psychiatric Treatment *that looked at risk assessment in OCD.*

ANXIETY AND ERP

When doing exposure therapy, it's important to recognize that anxiety is a normal, expected part of the process. If at first you don't experience at least a moderate amount, you're probably working on something that isn't sufficiently challenging. I don't want you to feel panic level anxiety. But the benefit from ERP comes from experiencing the anxiety and then having it diminish over time. Progress while doing this type of therapy is rarely linear. The goal is an overall downward trend, but sometimes you may notice that your anxiety starts to diminish, then you suddenly experience a spike. Fluctuation is to be expected.

The graph below demonstrates this process for Sharon, a client. She had a compulsion to touch the tops of her shoes. While she worked on the exposure exercise to diminish the act, her SUDS level initially shot up to a level 62. Then, after a while, it went down a little to 58, then spiked up again to 71. By the end of the exercise, a solid 60 minutes, it came all the way down to 21.

How any one individual will react to a specific exposure is often difficult to predict. For some their anxiety quickly subsides, but for others anxiety lingers. Be prepared for the unexpected, but remember you want to see an overall trend of lowering your SUDS level. By removing the compulsive actions, you will notice the anxiety that your compulsions are trying to block. Exposure therapy isn't really about you truly facing feared situations but rather about confronting the anxiety associated with them. There's a big difference between the two. I encourage you to let the anxiety come. Even embrace it. It will eventually diminish as long as you disengage from the compulsions.

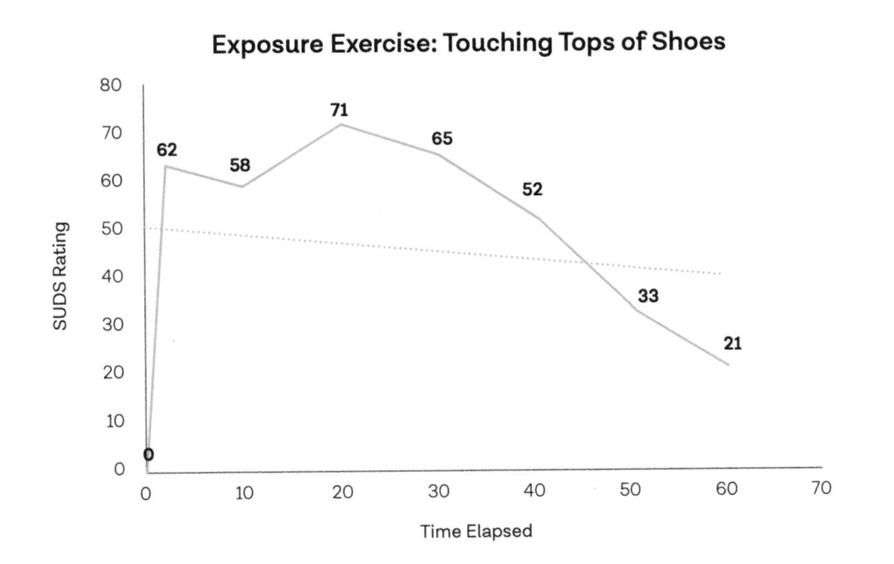

Practicing Exposure Therapy

At this point in the workbook, I'd like to review your first hierarchy. Have it with you as you read this section. I'm going to revisit some of the hierarchies I discussed earlier, plus others we haven't looked at before. Then I'll take you through a step-by-step guide to how to conduct exposure therapy with the listed items. This will help you do the same with yours.

The first three examples are personal hierarchies from my clients I've talked about in the book: Patrick, Michelle, and Catherine. The last two hierarchies are attached to specific obsessions. You'll see throughout I've also included some helpful ERP tips to guide you through the process.

Patrick's Fear of Fire Hierarchy

1. Use the washing machine with the water temperature set to hot. Do this without periodically checking to see if the machine is getting too warm or any other indication that a fire could start.
   ERP tip: Put a normal amount of clothes in the washer. Turn it on and walk away. Return only when the wash cycle is complete. Take the clothes out and put them in the dryer. No touching parts of the washing machine to check if it is hot.

2. Turn off light switches quickly and without placing them firmly down. Walk away without looking back at them.
   ERP tip: Make sure the light switches are left in a way that makes you feel anxious. Don't look at them again for several hours.

3. Turn off each TV while it is on a random channel, just not on channel four.
   ERP tip: Do this each time you turn off the TV. This should be done when you are actually watching TV and at other times when you're doing it solely to practice ERP. If you do this only when you want to watch TV, it will limit the amount of times you'll practice exposure therapy.

4. Turn off the computer and walk away from it. Do not place a hand on it to feel for warmth.
   ERP tip: Make sure to place the computer on a surface that may heighten your fear, such as a wood table. Return to it only after a minimum of two hours.

5. Use the vacuum cleaner for at least five minutes, then place it directly in the closet. Do not carefully check to see if it's touching anything else.
   ERP tip: When placing the vacuum back into the closet, make sure it touches other items. Don't delay putting it back in the closet. Do it immediately after use.

6. Cook something in the oven. Turn it off, and do not put your arms into the oven periodically to check the warmth.
   ERP tip: Purposely think that the oven may still be on and eventually cause a fire. Avoid looking at the oven light to see if it is on.

7. Cook something in the microwave. When it's done, remove it, and close the door. Don't reset the microwave for 10 seconds to check that it is actually off. Also, walk away from the kitchen to avoid any visual checking of the microwave.
   ERP tip: Purposely think that the microwave did not shut off properly and may cause a fire that destroys your apartment.

8. Use the toaster oven to make toast. Turn it off once, and leave the apartment within the hour without checking to make sure the oven is off.
   ERP tip: Make sure to leave the toaster oven plugged in. Purposely think about it causing a fire and destroying the apartment and injuring family members.

9. Boil some water with a stove top burner. Turn it off one time and without any counting.
   ERP tip: Make sure to walk away after turning off the burner. Also, don't check other burners. Purposely have thoughts of your family being hurt.

10. Make some coffee. Once it's done, turn the coffee maker off and walk away from the kitchen, leaving the coffee maker plugged in.
    ERP tip: Don't check whether the coffee maker light is on. Walk away and have thoughts of your family dying in the fire that was caused by your negligence.

Michelle's Contamination Hierarchy

1. Drive the car and do so without wearing gloves.
   ERP tip: Make sure to touch the car doors, and not just with your fingertips. Also, grasp the steering wheel without using any avoidance, such as the backs of your hands.

2. Pick up the kids from school and walk to their classrooms without wearing gloves. Be sure to touch the doorknobs, backpacks, books, and other items that may have been in the classroom.
   ERP tip: Look for items to purposely touch instead of waiting for them to surface—i.e., if the door is already open, touch the doorknob anyway. No avoidant activity when you're back in the car.

3. When putting the kids in the car, don't use hand sanitizer on you or them.
   ERP tip: No hand sanitizer before getting in the car or while in the car. Don't tell the kids not to touch items you worry may be contaminated in the car.

4. Have you and your children remain in the same clothes all day, and don't immediately wash the clothes they wore to school as soon as they get home.
   ERP tip: Allow your kids to play anywhere in the home. No choosing only certain rooms designated as contamination "safe" rooms.

5. Go food shopping without first cleaning the handles of the cart and without wearing gloves.
   ERP tip: Make sure to touch items you pick up at the store with your hands after fully touching the shopping cart handles. This includes fruits and vegetables. Leave your gloves at home.

6. While shopping, take the first items you see on the shelf. This includes cans and boxes. Don't grab items in the back that you assume are less likely to be touched.
   ERP tip: No closely examining items, such as cereal, before selecting, unless they appear to have been opened. Don't ask store clerks if items are safe.

7. Once home, do not scrub the fruits and vegetables with soap prior to putting them into the refrigerator.
   ERP tip: Put items from the store directly into the refrigerator. Rinsing with water for a few seconds is permissible.

8. Go to the mall without wearing gloves, and make sure to touch at least 10 items during your visit without cleaning your hands.
   ERP tip: Items should be touched thoroughly and not just with your fingertips, the backs of your hands, or while covering your hands with clothing. These items should include doors, escalator handrails, and shopping carts. Touch your face afterward.

9. When in the mall, talk to a sales clerk and afterward shake that person's hand. No handwashing or use of hand sanitizer is allowed.
   ERP tip: Don't be selective about whom to ask or zero in on someone you feel may be less contaminated than others. Don't use hand sanitizer when you return to the car. Touch your face afterward.
10. Allow your children to go over to a friend's house. When they return home, do not change their clothes.
    ERP tip: Allow your kids to choose the friend they want to visit, not based on your assumption of which house appears to be less contaminated. Give each of your kids a hug when they come home without washing yourself afterward.

Catherine's Harm Obsessions Hierarchy

1. Watch the news on TV without putting the TV on mute when a story with violence comes on.
   ERP tip: Do so without any mental rituals, such as praying. Don't look away from the TV if a disturbing story is shown.
2. Write the words *kill*, *murder*, and *death* on pieces of paper and leave the papers where they will be seen frequently throughout the day.
   ERP tip: Write the words legibly and put them on at least 10 different pieces of paper.
3. Look at knives on the internet for five minutes at a time.
   ERP tip: Start with smaller kitchen knives and move up to butcher knives.
4. Look at knives on the internet for five minutes while also thinking to yourself that you could lose control and stab someone.
   ERP tip: Again, no praying while doing this or looking away from the screen.
5. At home, take a steak knife and put it where you can see it while watching TV.
   ERP tip: The knife should be located where you could reach it without getting up. Make sure to look at it frequently while watching TV.
6. At home, take a steak knife and hold on to it while watching TV.
   ERP tip: Hold the knife in a way that it is facing toward someone. If no one is at home, hold it while looking at a picture of family members.

7. At home, take a steak knife and hold on to it while watching TV with family members.
   ERP tip: Sit next to a family member on the couch, holding the knife with the hand closest to them.

8. At home, take a steak knife and hold on to it while watching TV with family members and purposely think about stabbing them.
   ERP tip: Same as number seven, but this time purposely have thoughts of stabbing that person. No praying or saying to yourself "just kidding."

9. Read a story in the news about a murder and insert your name each time the name of the perpetrator is used.
   ERP tip: Look for a story that refers to the person having lost control. Again, no mental rituals.

10. Write out a story about losing control, stabbing someone, and eventually having to spend the rest of your life in prison.
    ERP tip: Make it about one typed or handwritten page. Add that you will die alone in prison, since your family will have abandoned you out of shame years earlier. (This type of writing exposure will be explored in more detail in the next chapter, when imaginal exposure is described.)

Scrupulosity Hierarchy (Nonreligious Type)

1. Watch a TV show or video about stealing.
   ERP tip: As you watch, make sure to say to yourself that you enjoy it and would like to do the same.

2. Begin walking into a crosswalk after the red hand signal has appeared.
   ERP tip: Take your time. Don't rush through it.

3. Ride an elevator and push two floor buttons.
   ERP tip: Do this when a stranger is in the elevator with you. Don't apologize.

4. While at the grocery store, handle some fruit and leave it there. Don't take it with you just because you touched it.
   ERP tip: Don't wipe the touched fruit in an attempt to clean it. Also, don't place it in a position where you feel it is less likely to be touched by someone else.

5. Go to a bookstore or library. Pick up a book and put it back in a different location.
   ERP tip: Don't tell the store clerk or librarian where you put the book. Tell yourself that someone may not find the book they want because of your inconsiderate act.

6. Take home some pens and pads of paper from work.
   ERP tip: Don't confess to coworkers or bring them back the next day.

7. While at work, write your boss an email with some work-related question. Do so without saying "thank you" at the end of it.
   ERP tip: Don't go talk to your boss right afterward to gauge if she's upset with you for not saying "thank you." Don't show the email to a coworker first to see if it is acceptable.

8. Also at work, take home a magazine from the waiting room.
   ERP tip: Don't tell your coworkers that you've done this, and don't apologize to your boss or anyone else.

9. When on the freeway, drive five miles per hour over the speed limit.
   ERP tip: Do it for at least several miles, and don't confess this to family and friends.

10. Throw away some recyclable items in the regular trash container.
    ERP tip: Do this every day for one week. Make sure it's at least one item per day.

Sexual Obsession Hierarchy

(in this case, fear of being attracted to young children and family members)

1. Look at magazines with pictures of young children.
   ERP tip: Purposely have thoughts about these children being attractive. No mental rituals, such as telling yourself that you don't really feel that way.

2. Watch videos of young children.
   ERP tip: Tell yourself that you're enjoying it, and that it's the first step to actually becoming a pedophile.

3. Sit at a playground when there are children present.
   ERP tip: Tell yourself that you are enjoying watching these children and that you wish you could touch them.

4. Give a parent or sibling a hug.
   ERP tip: Give a full body hug. No half hug, such as using just one arm to barely touch the other person.

5. When playing with your young children, let them sit on your lap if that's what they want to do.
   ERP tip: Try to avoid checking to see if you're experiencing any signs of physical arousal. Keep in mind that doing so would be similar to thinking about having lice and suddenly noticing your head itch. You in fact might notice some mild sensations with a child on your lap and misinterpret those as signs of arousal.

6. Change your infant child's diaper.
   ERP tip: Don't avoid touching the child's private areas. Change the diaper just as someone would do who doesn't have this form of OCD.

7. Change your infant child's diaper while purposely having thoughts of wanting to touch them inappropriately.
   ERP tip: No mental rituals, such as telling yourself that this is just an exposure exercise and that you really don't feel that way.

8. Give your infant child a bath.
   ERP tip: As in number six, wash the child as someone without this form of OCD would do. Don't ask your partner if doing so is okay.

9. Give your infant child a bath while purposely having thoughts of wanting to touch them inappropriately.
   ERP tip: Tell yourself you're enjoying these thoughts. No confessing to your partner.

10. When in the presence of female family members, purposely briefly gaze at their breasts.
    ERP tip: Tell yourself that you're enjoying it and that you wish you could see them naked.

Now It's Your Turn

Now that you've reviewed multiple different hierarchies, it's time to work on one of your own. Before getting started, you'll first need the OCD fear thermometer and one of your hierarchies. As you get started, please use the worksheet below. Make copies for yourself for additional exposures. It's also fine to adapt one for yourself or put it in some digital form, as long as it has similar components.

You'll notice that we're checking your SUDS score every 10 minutes. For example, when Michelle gave her kids a hug, she also gave herself a SUDS score. She started with a rating of 85, then every 10 minutes I asked her to assess her score again. This was done over a period of one hour. During this time, she could do whatever she wanted, as long as it didn't involve any avoidance or any other type of compulsion. Once she reached the one-hour point, she no longer needed to use the worksheet, but she was still asked not to engage in any compulsive acts associated with this exercise. You can see that at about 20 minutes, Michelle experienced a brief spike in anxiety. As was discussed earlier, this is very normal. Don't be disappointed if that happens to you. Hang in there with it, and you'll notice the anxiety fade over time. Time is on your side. The longer you go without doing the compulsions, the greater the likelihood that the urge to do so will diminish.

Here's what Michelle's worksheet looked like by the end of the exercise. Blank worksheets follow for you to practice on your own.

MICHELLE'S ERP WORKSHEET

DATE/TIME	ERP PRACTICED	SUDS RATING	OBSERVATIONS
Thursday, 4 p.m.	Gave kids big hugs when they returned home. Used both arms. Our bodies were touching.	Initial: 85	At first I wondered if I could manage, but it was really okay.
		After 10 mins: 75 After 20 mins: 87 After 30 mins: 54 After 40 mins: 44 After 50 mins: 32 After 60 mins: 24	The next time I do this, I think it would be better to allow the kids to go to Andrea's house first. Her place always seems especially dirty to me, so giving my kids hugs afterward would be harder. This exercise was challenging at first, but the more time that passed the easier it got for me.

ERP WORKSHEET #1

DATE/TIME	ERP PRACTICED	SUDS RATING	OBSERVATIONS
		Initial: After 10 mins: After 20 mins: After 30 mins: After 40 mins: After 50 mins: After 60 mins:	

ERP WORKSHEET #2

DATE/TIME	ERP PRACTICED	SUDS RATING	OBSERVATIONS
		Initial: After 10 mins: After 20 mins: After 30 mins: After 40 mins: After 50 mins: After 60 mins:	

Wrap-Up

Congratulations! You've done your first exposure exercises. You've put in a lot of work getting to this point. It takes a lot of courage to confront your fears, and that's especially true in the beginning when you're not really sure what to expect. Don't forget that doing these exercises needs to be a daily activity as you work through your various hierarchies.

How did it go? Was this easier or harder than you were thinking it might be? Please write your thoughts below.

Did you learn anything new about your OCD? About yourself? Did anything surprise you during the exposures? Are there some things you feel that you need to do differently during future exercises? Please write your thoughts below.

STEP FOUR

Imaginal Exposure Therapy

I USE THIS EXERCISE FREQUENTLY with my patients as well as my students. I've heard it referred to in many different ways, though most often it's called the "polar bear" or "white bear" exercise (Wegner et al., 1987). Sit quietly for a few moments without any distractions around you. Now, think of a polar bear. Get a really good image in your head of this giant furry, white creature. Maybe think of it walking over ice and snow. Let these thoughts come for a few more seconds. If it helps, keep your eyes closed. Now, stop thinking of the polar bear.

How long did you last without thinking about it? A few seconds? If so, you're in some good company. I've seen a few people resist the polar bear thoughts for a few minutes, but it takes a lot of work to keep yourself that distracted. Most people either think of the bear immediately after I ask them to stop or at least within a few seconds.

Of course, it's not the bear itself that's important here. The idea is to show you that it's nearly impossible for most people not to have certain thoughts. Telling yourself not to think something typically has the opposite effect: You'll think about it even more. This is why using a technique called "thought stopping" is not recommended for OCD. Thought stopping is exactly what the term suggests. One popular strategy for thought stopping is to wear a rubber band on your wrist, and each time an obsessive thought surfaces you snap the rubber band and say out loud, "Stop!" The idea is to train you to stop having a given thought. As you'll see later, that strategy is the opposite of what's recommended for people who purposely have intrusive thoughts.

In my experience, people who use the thought stopping methodology as a means to control intrusive thoughts only end up with sore wrists. It's better to let the thought or image be present or to conjure it on purpose. Those thoughts are there anyway, so let's just use them to your advantage and beat OCD at its own game. The less you try to resist, the more quickly the disorder will lose its power. This way of treating OCD may seem counterintuitive. I recognize that most people would prefer to avoid bad thoughts. They can cause great torment. But, as you'll soon see, it's actually a very effective way of pushing back on OCD.

In this chapter, we will explore the exposure technique called "script writing." This involves taking horrible obsessions and turning them into a short story. Here you get to tell stories about terrible things you fear could happen to you, loved ones, or maybe even strangers. Like other exposure exercises, script writing will generate some anxiety followed by considerable relief. It's going to require you to practice your creative writing skills, which is one reason why I like it so much.

Shaun: A Case Study

Shaun is a 45-year-old auto mechanic who has had OCD since he was a teenager. Earlier in his life he had contamination fears associated with becoming seriously ill, though in more recent years the obsessive focus shifted to religion. Shaun grew up Catholic and continues to be active in his church, attending Sunday services with his wife and their three children, and a weekly Bible study. He also has terrible fears about going to hell, being gay, and becoming a pedophile. Seeing items such as clothes and furniture that have the color red in them often will trigger thoughts of the devil; seeing a gay couple will bring on obsessions of wondering if that is what he wants for himself; and seeing images of a young girl will cause fears of one day becoming a child molester. He had many other obsessive thoughts and images, and for Shaun they revolve around one central fear: going to hell. His primary compulsion is praying and doing so repeatedly throughout the day. His compulsions have made him late for social events and work meetings. He once missed his nephew's wedding because he felt that he couldn't leave his house until thoughts of the devil subsided. By the time he did leave, the wedding was over.

As Shaun and I discussed exposure therapy for OCD, I explained that writing a story about some of these fears becoming true could help ease his emotional pain. He wasn't happy with that idea and told me that having any such thoughts was against his religious beliefs. I told him he was having the thoughts anyway and that thinking about them on purpose could eventually weaken them. He decided instead to pursue therapy that didn't involve exposure work, but that involved exploring issues about his upbringing. His hope was that it could shed some light on his obsessive worry. All very interesting, but the obsessions persisted. He called me back six months later with a renewed interest in the therapy I initially had suggested.

Even though Shaun showed a renewed interest in the type of therapy I proposed, he was still reluctant to participate in even the mildest exposure exercises. I suggested that we meet with his priest, Father Thomas. The priest had taken confession from Shaun during times when he was overwhelmed with fear, so the father was familiar with OCD. My goal was for Father Thomas to give Shaun permission to participate in the OCD therapy. Father Thomas endorsed doing the therapy by explaining that God understood that Shaun has OCD and knows that his intrusive thoughts and images are due to the disorder and not a reflection of his actual beliefs. Shaun eventually, albeit reluctantly, decided to give it a try.

Shaun and I worked on the first exposure script together in session. He told me as much as he could about his fears, and I put it down on paper. I wanted to know everything I could about these thoughts and in as much detail as he was willing to tell me. In so doing, I learned that while going to hell was the ultimate punishment, Shaun also feared losing his job, going to jail, and his family abandoning him.

Shaun's Imaginal Script

I consider myself a highly religious person. Being Catholic has always been the most important part of my life. I love my wife and my three kids, but God is always first. Then why do I have these awful thoughts about young children and sometimes think about becoming gay? I even sometimes think that the devil is good, and God is evil. I don't believe any of it, but maybe I do. No, that just can't be true. I don't want to believe it. But I'm really only kidding myself, aren't I? I'm having these thoughts for only one reason: I do reject God. He's never really been important to me. I may go to church a lot and participate in Bible study, but it's all been just because I wanted that for my family. It was never really important for me. I've been a phony all these years. People think church is a meaningful part of who I am, but it's the devil that's really the most important. It's good, and God is bad. God can't be trusted. No one should ever put their faith in him. What has he ever done for me and my family? Nothing. My time at church has been a waste. I'm glad I'm finally able to accept these thoughts. It's been terrible all these years hiding my true feelings. What a relief to finally acknowledge all this. I know I'll never be permitted to attend this church and the services again, and the many friends I've had there will want nothing to do with me. My wife and my kids? They'll never accept this, either. I'll bring shame to all of them. So what? Isn't it more important to be true to what you believe is right? That's what I was always taught by my parents. Okay, now I'm certain. It's time to finally acknowledge that I no longer need God in my life.

Once I finish a script, I always ask my clients to assess how closely it describes their fears. Shaun's script clearly set off a tremendous amount of anxiety for him. His initial SUDS score was 90. I asked him to read the script, read it again, and another time after that. By the third time, his SUDS was down to 75 but spiked back up to 87 shortly after that. I had him continue reading the script over and over again. He must have read it about 20 times in matter of 30 minutes. By his tenth read, I could tell that he was getting a little bored, which was reflected in his SUDS score dropping to 45. By the end of 30 minutes, it had come all the way down to 30. His anxiety was down significantly because he started to understand he really didn't believe any of what I had written. He even reminded me of what I had told him months ago when we'd first met: He was beginning to understand that having the thoughts on purpose made them seem less important.

Cassandra's Imaginal Script for Pedophile Obsession

Let's take a look at a different script. This time it's associated with fears of becoming a pedophile. Cassandra worked as a pediatric nurse, loved kids, and someday hoped to have some of her own. But she had a great fear of becoming a pedophile. This is the script she wrote to help her work through her obsession.

> *This girl must be around eight years old. She's come into the office for her annual before-school exam. I remember seeing her last year and wonder why I remember her since she wasn't my patient at the time. Then it hits me. I remember her because she's so pretty. She's just eight years old; why am I having thoughts about how pretty she is? Am I attracted to her? Of course I'm not. I then take the girl and her mother to the exam room and take her vitals, but I'm feeling really nervous. I wonder to myself, Why should I be so nervous? I've seen hundreds of little girls before. Then it hits me again as I realize that I'm nervous because I'd like to touch her, maybe even kiss her. That's just not me. That's stupid. It's sick. I'm having those and similar thoughts, but I can't help the way I feel. I begin wondering if I might get a chance to kiss her, and right at that moment her mother asks me where the bathroom is. I can't believe it. Here is my chance. Her mother leaves for a few minutes, so I go to sit next to the girl on the exam table. I tell her she has pretty hair and lean over to give her a kiss on her lips. I then undo the tie in the back of her robe and begin caressing her chest. I have lost complete control, just as I feared I would. I can't stop myself. This little, innocent girl looks me right in the eyes as if to say, "You're scaring me. Please stop. Where's my mommy?" At that moment the exam room door opens, and her mother screams, "What are you doing?" She grabs her child and goes right to the office manager, my boss. I know it's all over by then. I am fired on the spot. I am eventually convicted of child abuse and spend some time in prison. I look for work for a few months after that but eventually decide to give up nursing since I can't find a job. I'm still unemployed. My family refuses to have any contact with me, and my boyfriend broke up with me as soon as he found out the real reason I left my job. I'm still in shock over this whole thing. I thought these were just obsessive thoughts and that nobody with OCD ever acts on their fears. I guess someone had to be the first, and that someone is me. I knew I couldn't be trusted with kids. I lost control exactly as I thought I would. I'll be paying for this for the rest of my life.*

Cassandra's experience was almost identical to Shaun's. Reading the script caused a lot of initial discomfort, but over time the anxiety associated with it significantly decreased. She really knew all along that she would never do any such thing, but she didn't believe it enough. Doing this exposure allowed her to realize that these fears were simply her OCD and nothing more.

Tim's Imaginal Script for HOCD

Tim is a married, 29-year-old psychotherapist who came to see me several years ago. While he already had some clinical experience with OCD in his work, he was not an OCD specialist. Tim lived in fear of becoming homosexual, which in clinical terms is referred to as HOCD. He wrote this script with my help.

> *I couldn't go out in public without wondering if some man I've never even met before is attractive. Whether it was at the mall, at work, shopping, or especially at the gym, I was flooded with these thoughts. Everywhere. I even looked at their crotches and butts. I usually looked away as soon as I noticed I was doing it, but I kept thinking that I wouldn't be looking in the first place if I weren't gay. I didn't think I was. I loved my wife, and we were expecting our first child later in the year. That's what I've wanted since I was a kid. I was so sick of having these thoughts, so I decided to finally see if they could possibly be true. One day I went to the gym with the goal of talking to this man who had come up to me a few times already. He seemed pleasant enough, and usually just wanted some assistance with the machines. So, instead of trying to avoid talking with him any longer than I had to, I decided to go up to him and strike up a conversation. His name is Rick. Seemed like a good guy. Works for a local start-up in some IT capacity. Has lived in the Bay Area for the past eight years, originally from Wisconsin. He then tells me he came here to be with his partner at the time, though the two have since split up. "Okay,* partner *can mean several things," I said to myself, but before I had a chance to think it through he referred to his ex-partner as "he." I was amazed. Not to learn that he's gay but that I was excited that he was now single. I was afraid of this all this time, and now I was feeling relieved to know that those feelings were real. Rick later asked me if I wanted to go watch the basketball playoff game with him, and I jumped at the chance. One thing led to another, and I eventually spent the night with him. I told my wife that I had been out drinking with the guys and thought it best to stay at Jack's place instead of driving*

home. She understood and was glad I was being safe. Well, she got a little suspicious when this happened three or four times that week and wanted to know what was really going on. I kept to my story until she saw a text from Rick. My marriage was over in a heartbeat, and so was my brief affair with Rick. It's now six months later, and our son, Bryce, is four months old. I get to see him every other weekend. My parents are still angry with me. Not so much for being gay but for how it all happened. I wish things were different. I'd like to see Bryce more often, and maybe someday I will. The one good thing in all of this is that I'm finally free to be who I really am.

This exercise helped Tim quickly gain some control over his HOCD. The distress he showed early on in this process had diminished quite a bit by the next time we met. As instructed, Tim reviewed his script for at least 30 minutes per day. He read it over and over again, and even though he got bored with it he just kept reading it. We both knew that these thoughts would still surface, but the difference after the exposure work was that they no longer resulted in this

THINKING WON'T ALWAYS MAKE IT SO

"Couldn't repeatedly having these types of thoughts make the feared circumstance come true or make me do something I don't want to do?"

I've heard this question many, many times, but I've never seen it happen or have even heard of it happening. Could it? I suppose it's possible, but it seems very unlikely to me. I don't mean to sound like a broken record, but I don't think so. What I often say to my clients is that they're suffering so much already that it's worth taking the risk to do the exposure therapy. It's much more likely that the exposure therapy will result in your healing than the feared circumstance actually happening. As was mentioned earlier, I've yet to see reports of someone with OCD doing what they actually feared. Could you be the first? I guess it's possible, but does the low probability of it happening really warrant all the compulsive activity and obsessive worry? I don't think so. Whatever minuscule risk there is of that happening, it seems like a risk worth taking if the end result is you outmaneuvering the OCD and reclaiming your life.

never-ending self-reflection of whether or not he was gay. Although Tim wasn't 100 percent convinced that he wasn't gay, that concern became so small that it was no longer worth worrying about.

I'd like to end this section with a brief postscript. People often ask about this form of OCD—basically, how can I be sure that this person has OCD at all? It's a good question, and I have two answers:

1. I'm not 100 percent sure. Can you say with 100 percent certainty that if you identify as heterosexual, someday you won't discover that you're gay, or if you're gay that you won't one day discover that you identify as heterosexual? None of us can. As was mentioned earlier, most people with OCD will recognize that their obsessive thoughts make little sense, yet they still focus on the 1 percent chance that it could be true instead of the 99 percent chance that it isn't.
2. I do recognize that the process of coming to terms with your sexual identity can sometimes be a difficult and emotionally painful experience. At some point, however, a person knows what feels right to them. In HOCD, as with other forms of the disorder, the obsessions are intrusive and unwanted and cause considerable distress. There's nothing pleasant about them. Of course, the OCD will often force someone to think, *Maybe I do enjoy this*. But there is a big difference between a thought and knowing for sure that your attraction to the opposite sex feels right to you. It's really not hard for someone who specializes in OCD to tell when something is OCD related versus when it isn't. If the thoughts or images weren't OCD, they wouldn't be so disturbing.

Guidelines for Exposure Scripts

Guidelines for exposure scripts are very similar to those for real-life exposures. However, keep these important factors in mind, which are very specific to these imaginal exercises:

Just like with real-life exposures, you can write scripts in a hierarchal fashion. You may choose to start with less worrisome obsessions and move on to those that provoke more anxiety. I find that the anxiety associated with scripts often takes less time to fade than the anxiety with real-life exposures, so I tend to move through the hierarchies for imaginal exposures faster. It is, however, on a case-by-case basis, so you have to judge what you're ready for.

Your hierarchies may include increased levels of responsibility and occurrence. In other words, start out writing about a situation you fear may happen or that could be your fault. Once the anxiety subsides, reframe the events in a way that they become increasingly more likely to occur and create greater amounts of anxiety. The idea is to continue with this process until the scenarios no longer cause you any significant distress.

Scripts don't have to be long, but they do need detail to capture the obsessive fears. I often suggest no more than one double-spaced typewritten page. As long as you accurately capture the fear and elicit enough anxiety, you don't need to overwrite.

Be creative, descriptive, and vivid in your writing. But don't write something that seems so totally implausible that you wouldn't find it worrisome.

Consider recording your script. In years past, some people would record the script on a cassette tape and then replay it over and over. Smartphones are perfect for this. Most phones have a recording app, and if yours doesn't, you can easily find one to download.

Review the script several times per day for at least 30 minutes each. Do this even if you become bored. If you're bored after 10 minutes, continue to listen to or read the script for the entire 30 minutes. I want you to get good and bored with it.

Don't allow yourself to get distracted in the process. If you find yourself thinking about other things during the exposure, make sure you refocus on the script or the recording. Some people have told me that this type of exposure doesn't work for them because it feels too artificial. I recognize that can be true, but more often the script doesn't work because the fear wasn't properly identified. Sometimes the script doesn't have enough anxiety-provoking information in it.

Use this process as a way to lead up to real-life exercises. This is especially true if tremendous anxiety exists. For example, if a person with fears about killing a family member can put together a script and review it until the anxiety begins to subside, I'd say a real-life exposure exercise is likely the next step. At that point, the person may be ready to hold a knife while in the presence of family members.

Imaginal scripts can help when real-life exposure is difficult to accomplish or inappropriate. Fears associated with endorsing the devil, for example, may be difficult to address with real-life exposures. The same would be true for existential OCD, where the fears have more to do with meaning of life issues. Obsessions associated with harm are often best done through imaginal work. I wouldn't suggest, for example, that a person with fears of speeding their car through a crowd of pedestrians to drive quickly through a mall parking lot to prove the point that they're not going to hit someone. However, writing a script of that scenario would likely be very useful.

Be especially careful to avoid mental rituals while doing exposure scripts. This includes praying, counting, saying neutralizing words or phrases to yourself, and statements such as "just kidding." They defeat the purpose of the exposures. I'm often asked how long it usually takes to significantly lower anxiety when using the scripts. I've seen some people immediately recognize the unrealistic nature of their fear, resulting in reduced anxiety. For some it can take up to an hour before their anxiety abates. Remember to practice patience. Different obsessions may take different amounts of time before your anxiety lessens.

Sometimes, patients say they worry that someone may find their script or recording. You may be wondering the same. I say write the script anyway. No one is going to think you actually believe what you have written or recorded. If you use a notebook to maintain your privacy, you could write "OCD homework" on the inside cover. If you're making a recording, you could call it "OCD harm obsession exposure script." Labeling your exposure work in that manner may help you to feel better about doing it. My only warning is that these labels or titles shouldn't become a form of reassurance. If taking these precautions makes you feel less worried about the obsession itself, then I would suggest you refrain from adding labels or titles. As long as the notes or titles don't interfere with the exposure therapy, I think using them is fine.

EXERCISE: IMAGINAL EXPOSURE SCRIPT

Can you think of an exposure script for yourself? Don't worry about making it perfect. Use the space below, or type a script on your computer or phone. Make sure you have the fear thermometer and ERP worksheet with you, since you'll need them to complete the exercise. You can also use the worksheet below.

IMAGINAL ERP WORKSHEET

DATE/TIME	ERP PRACTICED	SUDS RATING	OBSERVATIONS
		Initial: After 10 mins: After 20 mins: After 30 mins: After 40 mins: After 50 mins: After 60 mins:	

How did you do? What did you learn from this exercise? Did you discover anything new about your OCD and about yourself from this? Did you find it useful? Were you able to generate some anxiety? If not, any ideas about what you might do differently next time? Also, were you reluctant to write some thoughts? Why? Please write your responses in the space below.

Now that you've given this a try, can you think of other obsessions for which imaginal exposure might work? Did you come across any that you feel would be better served by doing real-life exposure? Please write your responses down in the space below.

___

___

___

___

___

___

___

___

___

___

___

___

Some people with OCD express concerns that once they no longer experience anxiety over their obsessive thoughts, they could become even more susceptible to acting on them. They believe it's the anxiety that keeps them in check. My response is to do the exposure work anyway. In my 29 years of practice, I've never seen a client who has successfully completed ERP, then acted on the very thing that they feared. If you believe that you have OCD, then you also need to trust the ERP process.

Wrap-Up

I can't say enough about how important creativity is to the success of your exposure therapy. I've said it before: OCD is a creative disorder, and we need to be even more creative as we go through the process of fighting it. The imaginal exposure scripts are the perfect tools. Plus, there's nothing wrong with having some fun while you're at it, either. The goal is to get you to the point where you can recognize how unreasonable these obsessions can be. Your story should be rooted in believability. If it's too far-fetched, it won't create enough of the anxiety that is needed to move forward in the healing process.

By now you've done some real-life exposure and imaginal exposure. What do you think? Have you found one more effective than the other? As we continue on this journey, what do you feel that you need to continue to work on? Is there anything you haven't addressed yet? Please use the space below to write your responses.

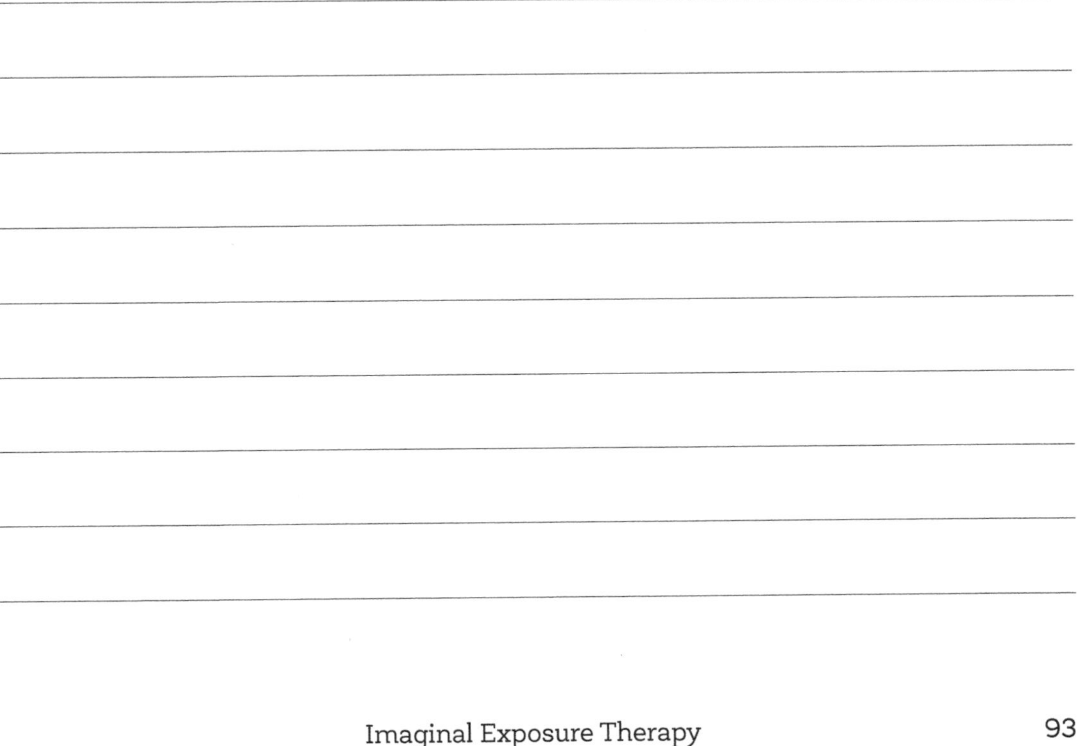

STEP FIVE

ACT and Be Mindful

IN MY EXPERIENCE, I have found some forms of OCD to be more difficult to treat than others. Those that tend to involve more mental rituals than observable, physical rituals often fall into that category. One such manifestation is sensorimotor OCD, which was briefly addressed in chapter 1.

One of my clients, Juan, had many different types of OCD over the years. Earlier in his life the disorder focused mostly on obsessive doubt and compulsive checking behaviors associated with locking up his apartment. As he got older, the obsessions shifted to fears about not completing various assignments for work. Certain letters couldn't be used together in the same word without his having to perform compulsive acts. All the effort involved in that often resulted in his missing important deadlines. More recently, the obsessional content was about swallowing. Juan explained that every time he swallowed, he consciously thought of doing so, which meant he thought of the behavior hours upon hours each day. He felt it disrupted every facet of his life: work, being with his wife and children, and whatever leisure activity he was engaged in—watching TV, reading, playing golf. Whatever he was doing, thoughts about swallowing were never far away.

Our first dabble into ERP involved Juan writing and reviewing his exposure script. It included his inability to stop thinking of swallowing so much that he had to quit work and go on disability. The script also incorporated his real obsessive thoughts, including his wife eventually filing for divorce and his kids becoming too frustrated to want to spend time with him. In the end Juan essentially loses all meaningful relationships in his life. Reviewing the script seemed to help him recognize the nonsensical nature of his worry. Still, the obsessional thoughts about swallowing persisted. We also tried exposure exercises, which involved him purposely having the thoughts about swallowing. If he noticed that the thoughts weren't present, he was instructed to start thinking about them. The goal was to essentially "burn out" the obsessional worry associated with thoughts of swallowing.

Another method, similar to what I described above, required him to leave Post-it notes in various places around his house reminding him to think about swallowing. The Post-it notes ensured he would gain constant exposure to the obsession. Some people have found this type of exposure for their sensorimotor obsessions to be very helpful. For Juan, it did contribute to some mild relief, as he did experience some lessening of the obsessional thinking. However, it did not last for long. His obsessive thoughts returned after a brief remission and were as intrusive as ever. Understandably, Juan was feeling very frustrated and expressed considerable hopelessness that this problem would ever get much better.

I suggested we try a different approach, which involved trying some mindfulness exercises. He assumed it was never going to work for him since he'd had some experience with it in college that wasn't particularly beneficial. Juan also knew that OCD was treated most effectively by using exposure therapy, so he had doubts. I explained that some of my clients, especially those with this form of OCD, found considerable relief in learning how to focus on the moment instead of on their obsessive thoughts. He was skeptical but decided to give it a try. It turned out to be the best intervention for him.

We reviewed various mindfulness exercises to teach Juan how to disengage from fighting with the OCD. When he thought about swallowing, he would focus on his breathing. He would acknowledge his thoughts about swallowing, but instead of dwelling on those thoughts he could go back to the breathing. It took Juan at least a month of daily practice, but eventually he became very good at it. Today, Juan is no longer particularly distressed over the swallowing obsession. What's more, he continues with his mindfulness exercises daily, knowing that the OCD can strike at any time. He also has told me that the practice has helped him develop a greater overall sense of well-being, providing him with benefits far beyond the relief from the obsessive preoccupation with his swallowing.

You may be concerned that focusing on one's breath might turn into an obsessive focus on breathing instead of being a useful mindfulness practice. While I've never seen it happen, I see no reason why it couldn't. But it actually doesn't matter. Once someone gets skilled at mindfulness, they will be able to successfully utilize those techniques to deal with any new obsessions that may surface. I believe the benefits associated with doing mindfulness far outweigh whatever risk there might be of new obsessions developing.

Why Mindfulness?

As I mentioned, it took me a while to come around on the usefulness of mindfulness in terms of treating OCD. However, mindfulness provides incredible benefits. Below are a few reasons why this type of practice is helpful, even for those who do not struggle with OCD.

Think Clearer

I often tell my clients that mindfulness is only partly about achieving a sense of calmness and relief from anxiety. Sure, those are common benefits, but so is the ability to think from a clearer perspective. Imagine how much more productive you could be in so many areas of your life—work, school, relationships, even fun

can be. Regularly practicing mindfulness can bring considerable relief to people suffering from OCD, just like it can with other anxiety-related problems.

De-stress

If you'll remember, I previously taught a stress management class for people experiencing a wide range of ailments, both physical and psychological in nature. At the end of each class, participants were given some homework assignments, one of which was to engage in at least one nurturing activity each day. People often talked about the benefits of some very simple activities, such as listening to music, gardening, reading, and exercising. During each class, we reviewed a mindfulness exercise, and this exercise was consistently reported as the most useful. Participants often described improvements in their mood, sleep, and concentration and a greater overall sense of well-being.

A Mindfulness Exercise

Let's take a moment and review a simple mindfulness exercise. With this practice, try to keep in mind that there is no way to "fail"; this practice is meant to be done without judgment. Be patient with yourself.

Expect your mind to wander, especially in the beginning. You may find yourself thinking about work, school, what you want for lunch, or plans for the weekend. Whatever the distractions, simply notice them, and then get back to the exercise. It's far easier to learn mindfulness exercises by listening to the instructions, so I encourage you to record this exercise. Record it yourself or get someone else to do it for you.

Lastly, you may find this exercise to be relaxing. While that's a good thing, it's not the primary goal of mindfulness. Try not to fall asleep. Maintain awareness of your thoughts and body, and develop the ability to disengage from the stress associated with whatever you might be experiencing. If you fall asleep, you won't achieve the desired result of learning how to mindfully deal with your obsessions.

Let's begin.

Sit in a quiet, peaceful place, in a comfortable chair or on a pillow or cushion on the floor. Choose somewhere that is free of distraction. Now close your eyes. Bring your awareness to how your body feels. Can you notice the sensation of your legs touching the chair or cushion? How about your arms? Are they by your sides or folded in front of you? Notice sensations with other body parts: your feet, knees, back, and shoulders. No judgments on whether you are doing this properly. Notice these various sensations. This time is for you. If you notice distressing thoughts surfacing, let them be, and return your focus to your body.

(Pause here for 20 seconds.)

Do you notice any tension in your body? In your back, shoulders, or other parts of your body? If the sensations prevent you from focusing, take a moment to adjust to a more comfortable position. If the discomfort is only slight, simply notice what you feel.

(Pause here for 20 seconds.)

Now let's turn to your breathing. As you take a deep breath, pay attention to the movement in your stomach and your chest. Can you feel your breath passing through your nose or your mouth and down into your lungs? Is it warm? Is it cool?

(Pause here for 20 seconds.)

Let's stay with your breath for a few more moments. Is there a rhythm to your breathing? If so, try to focus just on that and notice the in and out of each breath.

(Pause here for 20 seconds.)

Do you notice any new distractions? Are there any noises around you or any physical sensations? If so, don't try to push them away. Instead, acknowledge them and return to focusing on your breath.

(Pause here for 20 seconds.)

Let's get back to your breathing. Do you notice any sounds associated with your breathing? From your nose? From your mouth?

(Pause here for 20 seconds.)

Various thoughts, feelings, and physical sensations may pull you away from focusing on your breathing. That is normal and to be expected. Just bring your attention back to your breath. It may be helpful to calmly say to yourself "in" as you breathe in and "out" as you breathe out.

(Pause here for 20 seconds.)

Pay attention to the rising and lowering of your abdomen as you focus on your breath. Repeat "in" and "out" to yourself as you keep your attention focused on your breathing. In and out . . . in and out . . . in and out.

(Pause here for 20 seconds.)

Now, as we get ready to conclude this exercise, slowly open your eyes. Take a few moments as you gently allow yourself to adjust to your surroundings. Don't get up right away. Focus on the room around you and the sense of calmness you feel. Take this feeling with you as you reengage with the rest of your day. Keep in mind that your breathing is always with you and always available to help you achieve a greater sense of peacefulness. Please take a moment and reflect on how this went for you in the space provided below. What did you notice? Did you feel that you were able to concentrate on it? If you were distracted, were you able to get back to focusing on the exercise? Did you achieve some relaxation? Did you notice some tension? Do you feel that this type of exercise may have some benefit for you? If you didn't find it helpful, please also write about that. Are you open to continuing to try it? If not, please write about that as well.

Do you lose anything by practicing mindfulness daily for a week or two? I often say to my clients that there must be some benefit to the practice, given that it has been around for centuries and continues to be practiced by millions of people worldwide. Keep at it and you may find yourself pleasantly surprised. It's okay if you ultimately decide it's not for you—at least you tried.

A MINDFULNESS EXERCISE FOR OCD

Now, let's get back to my client Juan, who has sensorimotor OCD. Below, you'll find the mindfulness script I used for him. This is a much longer and more detailed exercise than the one you tried previously, but I've added some elements specific to help with his obsession associated with swallowing. You may find it helpful to mentally replace references to swallowing with the compulsion that you find the most troubling.

Sit in a quiet, peaceful place, in a comfortable chair or on a pillow or cushion on the floor. Choose somewhere that is free of distracting noises. Close your eyes. Bring your awareness to how your body feels. Notice the sensation of your legs touching the chair or cushion. Are your arms by your sides or folded in front of you? Notice sensations with your feet, knees, back, shoulders. No judgments on whether you are doing this properly. This time is for you. If you notice distressing thoughts about swallowing surface, let them be, and return your focus to other parts of your body.

(Pause here for 20 seconds.)

Do you notice any tension in your back, your shoulders, or any other part of your body? If the sensations are disrupting your focus, take a moment to adjust to a more comfortable position. If the discomfort is slight, simply notice what you feel.

(Pause here for 20 seconds.)

Now let's turn to your breath. As you take a deep breath, pay attention to the movement in your stomach and your chest. Can you feel your breath passing through your nose or your mouth and down into your lungs? Is it warm? Is it cool? Simply notice these sensations.

(Pause here for 20 seconds.)

Now I would like you to bring up thoughts about swallowing. Don't try to stop them. We know that's too hard to do anyway. Notice them. Let them be present. They aren't good; they aren't bad. They are just thoughts.

(Pause here for 20 seconds.)

Let's return to your breath for a few more moments. You may still be focused on your swallowing, but let's shift to your breathing. Is there a rhythm to your breathing? If so, try to focus on that and notice the in and out of each breath.

(Pause here for 20 seconds.)

If this is your first time practicing mindfulness, you may be wondering if you're doing it right. Allow yourself to be a beginner without judgment. Bring your focus back to your breath.

(Pause here for 20 seconds.)

What kinds of distractions are you noticing? Are there any noises around you or any physical sensations troubling you? Don't try to push away the distractions. If there are any, acknowledge them and return to your breath.

(Pause here for 20 seconds.) ▶

A Mindfulness Exercise for OCD, continued

Have you been thinking about swallowing? What types of thoughts have been present? Are you wondering if you'll ever be able to stop thinking about it? How it will affect your future? Let those thoughts be there. Resist any attempts at trying to reassure yourself. You know that hasn't worked anyway. These thoughts can't hurt you. They're just thoughts. Now, return to your breath.

(Pause here for 20 seconds.)

Do you notice any sounds associated with your breathing? From your nose? From your mouth?

(Pause here for 20 seconds.)

Various other thoughts, feelings, and physical sensations may pull you away from focusing on your breathing. That is normal and to be expected. Bring your attention back to your breath.

(Pause here for 20 seconds.)

As you breathe in, it may be helpful to say to yourself "in." Likewise, as you breathe out, say to yourself "out." In and out. In and out.

(Pause here for 20 seconds.)

Now let's revisit those thoughts about swallowing. Do they cause you some anxiety? You may worry about how they impact your job performance and your relationships. As you have those thoughts, shift your attention back to your breath. In and out . . . in and out. Your focus is on your breath.

Let's keep the focus on the rhythm of your breathing. Let thoughts, feelings, and physical sensations come, and let them go. In and out . . . in and out.

(Pause here for 20 seconds.)

What types of thoughts are you noticing now? Are they thoughts about swallowing, thoughts of calmness, thoughts of worry? Whatever they are, acknowledge your thoughts and let them pass without giving them any importance. Let them be, and focus on each inhale and each exhale.

(Pause here for 20 seconds.)

Pay attention to the rising and lowering of your abdomen as you focus on your breath. Repeat "in" and "out" to yourself as you keep your attention focused on your breathing. In and out . . . in and out . . . in and out.

(Pause here for 20 seconds.)

As you inhale and as you exhale, let your various thoughts come and let them go. Thoughts of swallowing are likely to be present. That's okay. Notice those, and return your attention to each inhale and each exhale.

(Pause here for 20 seconds.)

In and out . . . in and out. Keep your attention focused on your breath.

(Pause here for 20 seconds.)

Now, can you notice other sensations, such as your body touching the chair or your feet touching the floor? What about the smells around you or the taste in your mouth? Focus your attention briefly on those and then return to your breathing.

(Pause here for 20 seconds.)

Are you feeling tired, bored, irritated, sad, or frustrated? As with the other sensations, just notice those feelings and return to your breathing. Keep the focus on the in and out of each breath.

(Pause here for 20 seconds.)

Now, as we get ready to conclude this exercise, slowly open your eyes. Take a few moments as you gently allow yourself to adjust to your surroundings. Don't get up right away. Focus instead on the room around you and the sense of calmness you feel. If you're having troubling thoughts of swallowing or of anything else, they can't keep you from focusing on your breath. Take this feeling with you as you reengage with the rest of your day. Keep in mind that your breathing is always with you and always available to help you achieve a greater sense of peacefulness.

One of the challenges in treating OCD is that it presents differently in each person who has it. For that reason, a cookie-cutter approach to therapy doesn't work. Whether we're doing an ERP exercise or using mindfulness, it must be tailored to your own individual needs. As I mentioned, try this exercise on your own, but substitute your own statements about your specific obsessions. It's okay to take a moment to think about what you want to include. Include details of your particular obsessive thoughts as well as some desire to engage in, but ultimately resist, compulsive behaviors.

How was it? Did you find it helpful? Do you think this may be something you would like to keep doing? Please write your responses below. Also record if this exercise wasn't helpful. If you feel it would best to make some changes to the mindfulness script, please write about those, too.

____

____

____

____

____

____

____

If heightened anxiety has limited your ability to fully participate in exposure therapy, the use of mindfulness techniques may allow you to successfully reengage with ERP in a way that wasn't possible before. Plus, you may very well discover that the combination of mindfulness and ERP is more powerful than either used alone.

Accepting and Committing

In his 2006 report about ACT, published in *Psychotherapy in Australia*, Dr. Russ Harris describes ACT as "a mindfulness-based behavioral therapy that challenges the ground rules of most Western psychology. It employs an eclectic mix of metaphor, paradox, and mindfulness skills, along with a wide range of experiential exercises and values-guided behavioral interventions. ACT has proven effective with a diverse range of clinical conditions: depression, OCD, workplace stress, chronic pain, the stress of terminal cancer, anxiety, PTSD, anorexia, heroin abuse, marijuana abuse, and even schizophrenia." Harris believes the "goal of ACT is to create a rich and meaningful life, while accepting the pain that inevitably goes with it."

One of the more important factors in using concepts of ACT in managing OCD is to learn that the obsessions are simply thoughts, images, or urges. They carry no importance in and of themselves. The focus isn't on getting rid of them but rather learning to live *with* them and being committed to developing a life that is consistent with one's own set of values. Furthermore, don't wait for the obsessions and compulsive acts to lessen before you get on with your life. The idea is learning to accept their presence and building the life you want at the same time.

As stated previously, mindfulness is an important element within ACT. Another exercise that is useful for better managing obsessions is called "Leaves on a Stream." In ACT, this is known as a defusion exercise, in which someone learns to separate their thoughts and images from their interpretations. In ACT, our interpretations may contribute to our distress. Defusion allows someone to recognize that the thoughts themselves are not dangerous. They are simply thoughts, which don't have to result in experiences of distress if we just allow them to occur. The exercise is described below, as excerpted from the book *Get Out of Your Mind and Into Your Life: The New Acceptance and Commitment Therapy* by Steven Hayes and Spencer Smith:

> *Imagine a beautiful slow-moving stream. The water flows over rocks, around trees, descends downhill, and travels through a valley. Once in a while, a big leaf drops into the stream and floats away down the river. Imagine you are sitting beside that stream on a warm, sunny day, watching the leaves float by. Now become conscious of your thoughts. Each time a thought pops into your head, imagine that it is written on one of those leaves. If you think in words, put them on the leaf as words. If you think in images, put them on the leaf as an image. The goal is to stay beside the*

stream and allow the leaves on the stream to keep flowing by. Don't try to make the stream go faster or slower; don't try to change what shows up on the leaves in any way. If the leaves disappear, or if you mentally go somewhere else, or if you find that you are in the stream or on a leaf, stop and notice that this happened. File that knowledge away and once again return to the stream. Watch a thought come into your mind, write it on a leaf, and let the leaf float away downstream.

Now it's your turn. You don't have to purposely bring up your obsessive thoughts. Sit comfortably in a peaceful place, and let your thoughts come. As instructed in the exercise, let all your thoughts and images surface, neutral or filled with anxiety. Visualize each of the thoughts or images being on a leaf, and watch them all pass by. Do this for five minutes. When finished, make note of your reaction to it in the space below.

How was it for you? Were you able to watch your thoughts and images flow by? What types of thoughts and images did you notice? Did you notice any changes in the distress you felt? It may be difficult to notice much change your first several tries, so please keep at it. Try it every day for a week. Just like other mindfulness and defusion exercises, this, too, takes practice.

____

____

____

The Person in the Hole: A Metaphor

As noted previously, the use of metaphors is a central part of ACT. One of my personal favorites is the "Person in the Hole" metaphor used by Steven Hayes and Spencer Smith. In this metaphor, a person falls into a hole and is given a shovel to get out of it. But the hole gets bigger. Think of this metaphor in terms of someone trying to cope with OCD. If you try to figure out an obsession or actively try to get rid of it, the more problematic the obsession becomes. It's best to simply let it be and move on with things in your life that are more important. Of course, this all hinges on someone's willingness to consider that their obsessions may be meaningless. My advice is to let your thoughts be. Your thoughts are your thoughts; try to let them pass without placing any judgments either on them or on yourself for having them.

Use Different Types of Vocalizations

Another defusion strategy described by Hayes and Smith is "Create a Song." In this, you use your obsessive thoughts as the lyrics for a popular song or make up one of your own. For example, you could sing, "My house is going to burn down because I forgot to turn off the burner" to the tune of a song you know. Continue to do so until the words no longer carry much meaning for you. This is different from the process that was described in the section on imaginal exposure. In that, we repeat the exposure enough times so that your anxiety surrounding the issue eventually weakens. In defusion strategies, the goal is simply to recognize the obsessions as just words, as that may ultimately lead to a lessening of the distress associated with them.

What Are Your Values?

Understanding your values is another important concept in ACT because it can provide the motivation needed to change your relationship with OCD. The first step is to identify the values you hold deeply. This may not be as easy as it first appears. Fortunately, there are many exercises that can help you determine which values are most important to you. One such exercise is called "Attending Your Own Funeral." I know that someone with obsessive fears about dying may be cringing right now, but trust me, this isn't as morbid as it sounds. It's not an exposure exercise but rather one to assist you in determining whether you are living in a way that is consistent with your values. And if you aren't, this exercise can provide you with the motivation to do so.

As you've done previously, find a quiet, peaceful place to engage in this exercise. You'll be writing two eulogies. The first one will be what someone might say about you at your funeral should your life end with all of your current struggles intact. Think of all the ways your OCD has affected you: your relationships, work, and leisure activities. How has your OCD interfered with you fully engaging in so many other activities? It's likely that the OCD has influenced your decisions and ultimately prevented you from participating in a wide variety of minor and major life events. As examples, your list may include avoiding friends, an inability to leave home to attend your child's high school graduation, or never getting that promotion you wanted. Choose someone close to you to give that eulogy. Someone who is familiar with your struggles and who would give an honest assessment of how OCD influenced your life. Use the space below to write what that person might say.

____

____

____

____

I want to acknowledge that was likely not an easy task, especially if you allowed yourself to write an honest appraisal of your life with OCD. Before I ask you to write your reactions, let's write another type of eulogy. This time, life for you was different. Yes, your OCD was around, but you made the decision to fully engage in life anyway. You were able to recognize the obsessions as thoughts and images that passed through your mind without giving them any importance. You can choose the same person to write this new eulogy or someone else, but keep your focus on how your life may have turned out differently. Use the space provided below to write this eulogy.

____

____

____

____

Now let's take a look at how you did. First, I'd like to commend you for giving this exercise a try. Even someone without OCD may find it difficult to complete. How many of us truly are living lives consistent with our values? I'm sure we all strive for that, but an honest appraisal may sometimes prove otherwise. How was this for you? What thoughts and emotions were triggered? Was there some sadness, anxiety, anger, disappointment? If they were there, please make note of those reactions here. Of course, please also write about your values. Did this help you identify what is most important to you? Are you living in a way that is consistent with them? If not, how much do you think the OCD is interfering with that? Please write your reactions in the space provided below.

ACT-Enhanced ERP

As you might have realized by now, ACT doesn't focus on anxiety reduction. Rather, it's designed to teach how to live life with the presence of troubling thoughts and feelings. Instead of measuring anxiety as you would with an exposure hierarchy, ACT uses a willingness scale. The framework for this scale was detailed in a 2015 report published in *Journal of Obsessive-Compulsive and Related Disorders*. A score of 0 meant a lack of willingness to accept troubling thoughts and feelings without changing them, and 100 meant being completely willing to do so. ACT-enhanced exposure exercises work toward helping someone increase their willingness to live with the obsessions and to experience whatever uncomfortable feelings surface from not doing the related compulsive behaviors. At the same time, the person is also encouraged to pursue life in ways that are more meaningful and consistent with their values. In traditional ERP, the focus is on anxiety reduction as measured by the SUDS scale. In ACT, the focus is shifted to increasing willingness.

Let's take a look at the exposure hierarchy of my client Hallie. She has obsessive slowness, which we learned about on page 12. Remember, this is a form of OCD resulting in everyday behaviors taking long periods of time to complete. Hallie spends several hours engaging in behaviors, such as brushing her teeth and showering. This means she often sacrifices time she could have spent with friends or participating in other pleasurable activities, such as playing video games and watching YouTube. In addition, the obsessive slowness made her late for school and contributed to considerable tension between her and other family members.

OBSESSIVE SLOWNESS

When we talk about obsessive slowness, we're really talking about behaviors taking a long time. I treated a client who for several years showered only once every few months because of how emotionally painful it was to spend hours washing herself. The problem had little to do with contamination. Rather, she would get lost in her thoughts and lose track of where she was in her routine and have to start the process over every time when she realized what was happening. It wasn't unusual for her to take showers that were three hours long. Also, knowing that this occurred during California's terrible drought only made her feel even guiltier.

As a result of her obsessive slowness, much of her day was spent trying to either complete various activities or avoiding them altogether. Brushing her teeth often took 30 minutes, making her bed took 45 minutes, getting dressed took an hour, and getting ready for bed took about two hours. Understandably, she rarely went out and lost contact with most of her friends. There was no real routine to her days and no sense of day or night. Each day ran into the next, coming to an end only because of exhaustion. Truly, this was one of the sadder circumstances I have seen in my practice.

Her treatment included several components:

1. Reducing the amount of time spent engaging in these activities in a step-by-step manner. For example, when she started seeing me, her showers were often three hours long. She first reduced them to 90 minutes, then 75, then one hour, then 45 minutes, until she was able to reduce it to an average of 10 to 15 minutes. It took nearly two months to get the showering down to the 10- to 15-minute range.

2. Using a timer to keep tabs on her time. Whether this was in the bathroom or any other place at home, this client found it useful so she kept track of how much time she spent engaged in an activity. She was allowed a "two-minute warning" so that she still had some time to finish when the alarm sounded.

3. Previously, when she was in the bathroom, her parents and siblings would bang on the door, insisting that she speed up, which only made the anxiety worse. Family members now agreed to knock only once as long as my client acknowledged that she had heard them. They were also instructed not to continually badger her. This lessened the anxiety as well as some of the tension these behaviors often caused at home. The parents did, however, have the option of shutting off the water to the shower if she went over the agreed upon amount of time. Fortunately, it never got to that point.

4. Recognizing that the exposure was about not completing the activity to her satisfaction. This was the essence of the problem. She had to complete these activities in certain ways, and the amount of time involved often got out of control because of it. She had to accept that she was going to have to stop these behaviors, whether she was ready to or not. It wasn't easy. She often felt very frustrated stopping a behavior when it still felt incomplete, but she did it and eventually learned to speed them up in a way that ultimately allowed some sense of closure.

As we enhanced her hierarchy with elements of ACT, we included the potential benefits of doing the exposure exercises. She later told me that doing so increased her motivation to work on her OCD. As you review the hierarchy below, notice how it is influenced by her values.

100	*Limit the shower to 10 - 15 minutes to lessen conflicts with my parents over water usage.*
90	*Limit the time spent washing my face at night to 3 minutes so that my parents don't shut off the water.*
80	*Limit the shower to 15 minutes so that I can get to school on time.*
70	*After school, limit checking my homework to just once so that I have more time to do other activities during the day like play video games and go on YouTube.*
60	*When I'm in the shower, wash my hair just once so that I don't damage it any further.*
50	*When in the shower, wash my hands just once so that the skin will stop cracking from washing it so much.*
40	*Limit the time spent brushing my hair to 5 minutes so that I don't damage it any further.*
30	*Limit the time spent brushing my teeth to 10 minutes so that I can protect the enamel.*
20	*Limit the time spent getting dressed in the morning to 10 minutes so that I don't miss out seeing my friends before school.*
10	*Limit the time spent tying my shoelaces to 5 minutes so that I can leave the house without having to worry that I'm keeping everybody waiting.*
0	*Get up earlier on a weekend day so I can look for a summer job. Having one will give me some extra money to do more things with my friends.*

EXERCISE: ACT-BASED EXPOSURE HIERARCHY

Use the space provided below to put together a hierarchy not based on anxiety reduction but on your willingness to accept and live with those uncomfortable feelings and thoughts. Also include reasons why doing the exposure may be important to you.

100

90

80

70

60

50

40

30

20

10

0

What was this like for you? What differences did you notice compared to the hierarchies you did previously? Do you think this can be helpful for you? Do you find being able to identify your values helpful in this process? Please write your thoughts below.

Wrap-Up

With this chapter we shifted away from traditional CBT-based therapy to take a look at how both mindfulness and ACT can aid in your better coping with OCD. Neither is meant to be a substitute for ERP, though each offers ways to enhance the process. Imagine what it may feel like to simply allow all your obsessive thoughts to be present without either fighting with them or having them disrupt your day-to-day life. Both mindfulness and ACT can assist you in achieving that. Just don't forget the ERP components as well.

As we move forward, we'll discuss how to keep this all going. My hope is that you've seen some progress in dealing with your OCD. However, we aren't finished yet. It's important that we have a chance to review how you can keep moving forward. OCD isn't likely to stop harassing you, so we need to continue focusing on further strategies, even though you've already made some very significant changes.

How was this chapter for you? Do you feel that you learned some additional strategies to assist in better coping with your OCD? Do you feel there is more to work on? Please make note of everything here.

activities—if you didn't have all the mental clutter each of us lives with every day? Of course, none of us can get rid of all that entirely, but regularly practicing mindfulness exercises can help you to feel grounded, to stay in the present moment, and to keep you focused on what matters most to you.

Improve Memory

Besides our time at rest, we spend most of our days performing mental tasks, such as comprehending while reading, carrying on a conversation, doing a math problem, memorizing a telephone number, or recalling items on a shopping list. These are all possible because of our working memory, which enables us to maintain information long enough to engage in such mental tasks. I believe most people would say that they would like to improve their working memory if only they knew how. One way to do that is to learn mindfulness techniques.

Quell Obsessions

We'll get into this in more detail later, but for now it's important to mention the potential impact that mindfulness can have on limiting someone's obsessional thinking. As we know, one goal in treating OCD is to learn how to better cope with the obsessions rather than eliminating them entirely. That's not to say, however, that we shouldn't strive to lessen the distress associated with such thinking, because that certainly can be achieved. Staying in the moment is a key element of mindfulness and as such can be of great benefit to someone with OCD, as the obsessions are often about what may have occurred in the past or what could happen in the future.

Manage Anxiety

Anxiety comes in many forms. Most of us have normal experiences with anxiety, and anxiety also serves to protect us. Anyone who drives has had this experience: You're driving without any difficulty and suddenly notice another car come into your lane. You then quickly maneuver your car out of the way, avoiding a potential accident. We are able to do that because of anxiety. Sometimes, however, that type of anxious "fight-or-flight" reaction is triggered when it shouldn't be, such as when someone has a phobia or panic attacks. Of course, anyone who has OCD also knows how truly anxiety inducing the disorder, as well as the treatment itself,

STEP SIX

Keep It Going

WHEN TYLER AND I BEGAN WORKING TOGETHER, he had many intrusive thoughts about hurting infant girls. He especially had great difficulty being with his two young nieces. Every time they visited, he would have obsessions about hitting them with his fist. There were many times when he couldn't convince himself that he hadn't already done something. This contributed to tremendous feelings of guilt and shame and his avoiding having contact with them.

Tyler ended up doing very well with his exposure therapy, which often focused on being with his nieces and not doing any compulsions while in their presence, such as refusing to give them hugs. He also learned to accept the uncertainty involved. Tyler even got to a point where he was 95 percent sure that he wasn't going to do anything terrible to his nieces. The OCD wouldn't let him get to 100 percent certainty, but over time he learned to pay less attention to that 5 percent that was causing him trouble.

Tyler finished his therapy in about six months. I was very impressed with how aggressively he worked on his ERP exercises. By the time the therapy ended, Tyler had very few intrusive thoughts and was much less distressed when his nieces were present. But roughly five months later, I got a call from him because many of the thoughts had come back. Tyler once again was struggling to convince himself that he hadn't already hurt his nieces. He came back for two months. But this time, instead of just ending his treatment, we decided to meet once a month for a few months and after that once every few months. We did this so we could monitor his progress and catch any significant signs of the OCD returning before it got out of control. This is an important concept as we move forward and discuss various factors associated with relapse prevention.

So far, we've reviewed many ways for you to work on your OCD, including cognitive and exposure therapy. In this chapter, we will explore ways to maintain the progress you've made and how to avoid pitfalls that could contribute to relapse. It's first important to make the distinction between a temporary setback and a relapse. Temporary setbacks are to be expected. These are times when you notice an increase in your symptoms, but the occurrence is relatively brief. If you have OCD, it's likely that you will experience this. A return to using the ERP strategies you learned will typically resolve this. A relapse is more serious, as it is a prolonged period where the OCD returns in a way similar to what it was prior to your recovery. This may require restarting therapy and/or medication.

Once someone shows enough signs to warrant a diagnosis of OCD, they should expect to live with it in some form for the remainder of their lifetime. As discussed in chapter 1, the goal is to learn how to manage it and not to get rid of the disorder entirely. That's not to say, however, that people can't go for weeks, months, and even years without it causing trouble. Many people have. But to expect that OCD will be gone forever unfortunately will only set you up for grave disappointment. It's more realistic to plan for setbacks rather than to hope the symptoms never come back.

You may at times begin to notice an increase in your obsessive thoughts and more of an urge to engage in the compulsive behaviors you worked so hard at controlling. Not everyone will experience a full relapse, but the concepts of relapse prevention are important to review, since we want to do all we can to avoid that from happening.

Tyler experienced a setback in his recovery, but since it was fairly brief and not very severe, it didn't become a relapse. But why did it happen in the first place?

Stress is sometimes a trigger, but that isn't always the case. Tyler told me that life was in fact going quite well, so it was difficult to explain why this would happen. Was it some natural fluctuation within his brain chemistry that caused it? We'll never know. More important was that Tyler needed to once again participate in exposure therapy so he could get back on track. Below are various strategies that will aid you in either preventing relapse or mitigating the impact of one should it occur.

"Hope is not a strategy." This famous quote has been attributed to several people from the legendary football coach Vince Lombardi to Barack Obama. It's true for many facets of life, and it can be said for dealing with your recovery from OCD. As you begin to wind down the more structured part of this process, you will need to develop a plan for how to maintain the progress you've made. In my opinion, doing so is as important as all the work you did getting to this point.

Strategies for Relapse Prevention

The first step to take when you relapse is to understand what helped you during your previous treatment. Write it down. Record it in your phone. When Tyler had a setback, he began obsessing over the very same intrusive thoughts he had successfully worked on before. He questioned his reasoning that helped him let go of much of his obsessive worry and couldn't remember exactly what had helped him so much before. During his second episode of therapy with me, Tyler made notes on his phone. So the next times the thoughts started to pop up, he could easily remember that there were in fact times when he was very close to believing that he hadn't hurt his nieces in any way. The notes also helped him remember that he'd never done any such thing, that doing so would be abhorrent to him. Additionally, he wrote about how much various exposure exercises helped. The notes on his phone also aided him in recognizing that his thoughts were simply the OCD acting up, rather than some new evidence surfacing that proved he had committed some terrible acts.

Keep Up with Planned Exposure Exercises

Perhaps becoming complacent is human nature, but it's crucial to guard against doing so with your recovery. Doing ERP isn't particularly pleasant, but it beats falling into a relapse. Make sure you're doing planned exposures at least several times a week. If you're dealing with contamination fears, continue to touch some items you suspect will bother you without performing any cleaning rituals. If your issue has been symmetry, leave items out of place sometimes in a way you feel may cause you some discomfort. Whatever your form of OCD, maintaining planned exposure exercises is an important element in keeping your OCD under good control.

Let's take a short break here. What exposure exercises do you think you might need to keep up with? Please write those down in the space provided.

____

____

____

____

____

____

Stay Prepared for Spontaneous Exposures

As was discussed in step 3, you also need to be prepared for spontaneous exposures. This can be more important than the planned exposure exercises discussed previously. Life happens, and so does OCD. The disorder is always looking for opportunities to upset you. Too often I hear people say that they had an urge to engage in some compulsion and decided to do it that one time. The thinking behind that often is along the lines of *how much can it hurt if I just do it this one time?* The answer is plenty. You must remain vigilant and consistent. OCD will seek an opening, and when it finds one, that single act of compulsion can turn into two. Before you know it, OCD has taken over again.

MEDICATION AND THE "POOP OUT" EFFECT

The clinical term for this is "antidepressant tachyphylaxis," though it is often referred to as the "poop out" effect, according to a 2014 article published in *Innovations in Clinical Neuroscience*. This is when a medication that had previously been effective stops working. I have seen this occur at times with some of my clients. If you notice that you're having more trouble dismissing your obsessive thoughts and having more difficulty controlling compulsive behaviors, it may be time to consult with your psychiatrist again, especially if it goes on for more than a period of several weeks.

In my experience, however, it is far more common for a medication to keep its effectiveness over an extended period of time. Nonetheless, this occurrence is particularly significant when it comes to OCD, since many people may need to remain on medications for many years. You may hear clinicians use the term "wax and wane" when talking about how OCD presents itself. As has been previously stated, most people with OCD are going to experience moments when their symptoms worsen. This may not mean that the medication has stopped working, but rather it could just be an indication of the normal fluctuations associated with the disorder. However, if you find yourself in an episode that feels prolonged, you may have developed a tolerance to the medication, and it has lost its effectiveness for you. You may need to adjust the dosage, switch to a different medication, or possibly add another to augment what you are already taking. Try not to feel discouraged. In all likelihood, your doctor will have suggestions of other drugs that may work equally as well.

1. Do the best you can to anticipate stress. As was stated earlier, OCD, like so many other problems, will often react to stress, and that can contribute to an increase in symptoms. Whatever the stress—financial, relational, work, school, or something else—be aware that it may be a time when the OCD decides to cause you more trouble.

2. Practice healthy stress management. Regular exercise, maintaining a healthy diet, and getting plenty of sleep are all important, as is limiting use of alcohol or recreational drugs.

3. If you've been doing therapy, consider periodic checkup sessions instead of stopping your treatment altogether. Meet every other week for a while, then once per month, and then once every few months. If at that point you're still doing well, then it's time to discuss if therapy should be stopped for an indefinite period of time.

4. A setback may not require restarting therapy, but a relapse in all likelihood would. There's no shame in needing a refresher. You'd probably encourage a friend going through a similar episode to do that, so treat yourself the same way. Anyone who truly knows OCD knows this is a lifelong journey. People can go for extended periods of time when symptoms are very inactive, but it's likely to have some flare-ups on occasion. Hopefully you'll never get to the point of having a relapse, but one way you could avoid that happening is by addressing the situation with your treatment team as early as you can. ►

Medication and the "Poop Out" Effect, continued

What do you think? Are there any stressors you need to watch out for? What do you feel you could do to address them so they don't exacerbate your OCD symptoms? Are there other relapse prevention strategies you think may be useful for you? Please write your thoughts in the space provided below.

Don't Let Medication Stop You

If you're taking medication, don't fall into the trap of believing that you no longer need it because you feel better. Make sure you discuss stopping your medication with your doctor before making any such decision. It's very likely that the medication contributed to your improvement. To stop taking it before you and your doctor agree it's time to do so is unwise.

How Family and Friends Can Help

We've already established that exposure therapy is important in treating OCD. For many people, taking medications is also going to be a necessary part of the treatment plan. We've touched on other important elements as well, but what about families and friends? While they can't take the place of ERP and medication, an argument can be made that the role they play in someone's recovery may be every bit as important. Here are some helpful suggestions, both for you and for those to whom you are closest.

- Encourage them to read about OCD. Nothing is more powerful than information. You can find many good resources on the disorder, but none is better than the International OCD Foundation. The foundation provides a wealth of information on all subjects relevant to OCD.
- Family members are also scared. OCD is a disorder that forces people to have obsessive thoughts and engage in compulsive actions that make little or no sense. If it's scary to you, it's likely scary to them, too. While no one suffers more than the person who has OCD, friends and family also feel the pain the disorder can bring.
- Have an open dialogue about your OCD. Let important people in your life know what you find helpful and what isn't. If you're in therapy, consider having them attend some sessions with you. Your therapist can answer some questions they may have on how they might be best able to support you.
- Be aware of the pitfalls of asking for reassurance, as was discussed in chapter 1. It's important that you, your family, and others closest to you know what to do if you fall into asking for reassurance. It's so easy to ask sometimes, and since no one likes seeing you suffer, it can seem like the kind thing to do. But if people don't know not to provide reassurance, they will likely offer it up without knowing how counterproductive it really can be.

- Ask family and friends to attend an OCD support group. This can be with you or without you. The IOCDF website has listings of support groups located throughout the country.
- Family members may need their own therapy to better cope with their issues related to your OCD. They will be well served by seeing someone who specializes in the disorder.
- Make sure that they aren't participating in your compulsive rituals. Be careful not to ask, and they need to be careful to not engage, either. Just like offering reassurances, it may seem like the kind thing to do, but participating in your compulsions is anything but. For example, they shouldn't comply if you ask them to shower or buy more soap because you feel they're contaminated.

Advice for Families

OCD isn't anyone's fault. While it is recognized that OCD tends to run in families, this doesn't mean that it's your fault that you have it. It's really no different from a family member developing diabetes or heart disease. Thanks to extensive research, it's now widely accepted that the cause of OCD is largely biological and neurological and not due to some problems associated with parenting. It's not the fault of the person with OCD, either. You aren't being lazy or lacking willpower. The focus should be on you getting well while at the same time getting guidance for your family.

Getting mired in feelings of guilt or blame won't help anyone. It's much more productive for family members to learn as much as they can about OCD so that they have the facts about what is helpful and what isn't. As we have explored several times before, there are many pitfalls, especially in terms of providing reassurance and participating in someone's rituals. Family members need to pay close attention to avoiding those while at the same time being as compassionate to their loved one and to themselves as they can.

If you feel it may be helpful, ask a family member or friend to be your OCD coach, as was discussed in step 3. They, of course, will need some guidance from either you or a therapist, but I've seen considerable progress at times when a client of mine has someone who can serve as a coach. Remember, a coach needs to be understanding and supportive but also firm without being condescending. Simply reminding you to do your exposure therapy and offering some words of encouragement may be all that is needed.

Respect that your family has their own lives, too. This can be a tough one, but you don't want the OCD turning a household upside down. Sometimes they may leave for dinner without you if you've taken too long to get ready. Perhaps they use the remote control even if you've cleaned it and asked them not to touch it. Maybe they resist your compulsive attempts at asking repeated questions about what just happened on a TV show because of your uncertainty. Whatever the issue is, it's best for everyone that the household continues to operate as normally as possible. This may put extra stress on you at times, but try to think of it as a motivating factor for doing the hard work of exposure therapy. Being able to navigate all this can be very tricky for both you and your loved ones, and when that is the case it's best to have such discussions with a therapist present.

A sense of humor cannot be understated when it comes to dealing with OCD. While there really isn't anything funny about it, it doesn't mean that a good laugh isn't called for at times. However, it always needs to be done respectfully. It never means laughing at you or making fun of you. There's no place for that. But when coming from a caring place, a sense of humor can provide the relief that's needed sometimes. You're the best judge of this, though. If someone says something that is meant to be funny but turns out being hurtful, let them know.

When deciding if and when to reveal your diagnosis, my suggestion is to think about who needs to know and who will be supportive of you. The most challenging situations may occur on the job. The Americans with Disabilities Act protects people with OCD from being discriminated against in the workplace and allows for reasonable accommodations to be made for you so you can perform your job duties in a satisfactory manner. For further information on this, you may want to contact your HR division or seek legal counsel.

What are your ideas? What do you think your family and friends can do to better help you? Is there anything you feel you could be doing to help them? What about your work? Are there any special circumstances there that may need to be addressed regarding your OCD? Please write your responses below.

____

____

____

____

____

____

____

____

Wrap-Up

Relapse prevention and families: The two are often linked. OCD wants you to believe that something is important when it isn't. You may find yourself in the midst of obsessive thoughts and engaged in compulsive behaviors and be unaware that the OCD is getting the better of you. Caring families and friends can be of great help in pointing this out and may assist you with not falling into a relapse. I also believe that you have a responsibility when it comes to dealing with those closest to you. Don't be afraid to educate them, and encourage them to get their own help if needed. Additionally, I think it is important for you to acknowledge that they, too, suffer and that setting limits on your OCD is important not just for you but for them as well.

How has this chapter been for you? Do you feel that you've learned anything new about dealing with setbacks and relapses? How about with your family and friends? Are there any people you would like to tell about your OCD? Are there people you feel you shouldn't tell? Is there anything that hasn't been covered here that you feel the need to address? Please use the space provided below to write your thoughts.

CONCLUSION

AT THE BEGINNING OF THIS BOOK, I discussed the first person I ever met with OCD. It happened while I was working at a nursing home in San Francisco. While we never did any OCD therapy, I sometimes wonder what her life might have been like had she received the treatment that is now available. Would it have changed her life? We'll never know.

That same question can be asked of many people today who struggle with OCD. One of the reasons I decided to write this book was to offer hope. OCD is a tough opponent, but it can be managed with the right therapy. In regions such as the San Francisco Bay Area, where I work and live, it's not that hard to find OCD specialists. In the past five years, I've seen a tremendous change in the number of therapists specializing in OCD. Cost and appointment availability are sometimes difficult hurdles to overcome, but people here have many more options. I'm not sure that's the case for other parts of the country. I don't consider this book to be a substitute for therapy; I do think it can be a tremendous guide for those trying to better cope with their OCD, whether or not they are working with a clinician. If your therapist is not an OCD specialist, I encourage you to share this resource so that the two of you can learn and work on this process together.

I began by congratulating you for taking the courageous step of deciding to take back control of your life from the grasp of OCD. Now that you've almost completed this book, I'd like to once again congratulate you, this time on completing this part of your journey. Even though you're at the end of this book, in many ways this is just the beginning in the process of continuing to stay well. I know this hasn't been easy, especially as you've experienced the difficulties involved in confronting OCD.

One of the most challenging aspects in being an OCD specialist is trying to find ways to explain to clients that in order to get well, they'll need to experience even more anxiety than they already have. Under those conditions, who would ever want to seek this type of therapy if they didn't know the benefits of it? This is what makes treating OCD unlike treating many other disorders. For depression, the goal is not to have people become even more depressed before they get better; no one would ever return for a second session if that were the case. OCD is different. People engage in compulsive behaviors because they have learned over time that doing so aids in neutralizing their obsessive thoughts, at least for some brief periods of time. Of course, that strategy isn't sustainable and usually contributes to even more dysfunction. However, the compulsive behaviors do serve their purpose in that the anxiety caused by the obsessions is mitigated, at least temporarily.

In doing OCD therapy, people are essentially taught to fight fire with fire. You bring on the anxiety instead of trying to avoid it. Do so long enough and the anxiety associated with it begins to subside. If you have multiple obsessions, it's crucial that you repeat that tactic while disengaging from your compulsions until you've gone through all items on your hierarchy. While this can be incredibly challenging, I do hope that you've also seen that the goal is to exhaust the OCD, not you personally. The treatment is always a step-by-step process, so tackle only items on your hierarchy that you feel ready to confront. Yes, we need to be reasonably aggressive, but you shouldn't feel too scared to move forward with the therapy. Adding cognitive therapy skills along with mindfulness and ACT can serve to make this process more manageable. It's my preference to utilize as much ERP as possible. Hopefully you're at a point where you understand that multiple strategies are often necessary to achieve the ultimate goal: to lessen the torment often caused by this unrelenting disorder.

As I have often said during speeches to various organizations and to my students, I have tremendous respect for people who have OCD. Getting better takes persistence and dedication. Just when you think that you've got it under control, OCD will throw you a curveball. That's why I don't discuss eliminating OCD entirely. Instead, I place an emphasis on learning the various CBT skills so that you can deal with OCD episodes as they reoccur—because they will, time and again. My hope is that by reading and completing this workbook you've learned these skills, or that the book has enhanced what you already know.

Workbooks are meant to be your guides through your recovery process. When treating a client, I frequently reference the workbooks I own, showing them sections that I have found especially useful. I would like you to use this book in the same way. It's not meant to be a one and done experience. Reread it as often as is necessary, and certainly use the worksheets to guide you through your exposure experiments. One hope I had in writing this book was to join together the state-of-the-art treatment strategies while also personalizing it to meet individual needs. The book is meant to be written in, but if your OCD involves not wanting to write in books, use this as yet another way to do exposure therapy!

I'd like to conclude with a story about a former client of mine. Courtney was in high school when she started treatment with me. She missed much of her junior year because of her OCD. She had severe contamination fears, among others that interfered with studying and disrupted her social life, so much so that friends stopped contacting her. Her parents had tried some therapists, but they weren't OCD specialists. Then they found me. I referred Courtney to a psychiatrist for medication, and that did provide her with some much-needed relief. The real work, however, came when we began exposure therapy. It took her almost a month to agree to it, but once Courtney got the hang of the process she made big improvements. Sure, there were some setbacks along the way, but she persisted. Two steps forward, one step back. Sometimes it felt like two steps back, but the important takeaway is Courtney never gave up.

Fast-forward 11 years. I ran into Courtney at our local supermarket. She was with her one-year-old daughter and her mother. I couldn't believe it—she had a daughter! There were times during our sessions when she couldn't even get out of bed due to her multiple fears associated with contamination. But that day I learned she was married, had a child, and had worked at a software company before taking an extended maternity leave. We exchanged some pleasantries at the store, but to protect her privacy in a public setting, I didn't mention anything about her OCD. As I walked away, I saw her running back toward me while still holding on to the shopping cart.

"Do you notice anything different?" she said, laughing.

Well, I did notice that she had a baby, but that wasn't what she had in mind.

"Look at me. I'm food shopping, holding on to the disgusting handle of this disgusting shopping cart, and even had my daughter sit in it! The best part? I couldn't care less!" she said. "Thank you for saving my life."

And with that, Courtney smiled, grabbed the shopping cart one more time, and walked away.

I know several of my colleagues have had similar experiences. It's one of the joys of doing this work. Seeing someone get well and build a productive, happy life for themselves, and knowing that I had some part in that happening, is beyond gratifying. But, truthfully, I was just Courtney's therapist, a guide for her journey. Yes, we worked together on her recovery every step of the way, but she did the heavy lifting. She had the courage to do the hard work and to keep going when it would've been so much easier to succumb to the OCD.

Courtney's story is heartwarming and encouraging. But it's also not unique. I've watched many people with OCD take control of the disorder and improve their lives and livelihoods, whether through my own work or my involvement with OCD SF Bay Area or the IOCDF. I wouldn't have agreed to write this book if I didn't know it was possible.

So, please, read this book and read it again. Use the worksheets. Keep at it, especially at times when you feel that the OCD is winning. Perseverance. Courage. Resilience. OCD is no match for these traits. Please keep up the fight. I know you can do it. It's worth it. And if you happen to see me at the supermarket, please say hello.

RESOURCES

- The Anxiety and Depression Association of America, ADAA.org
- Beyond OCD, BeyondOCD.org
- Headspace, Headspace.com
- The International OCD Foundation, IOCDF.org
- National Alliance on Mental Illness, NAMI.org
- National Institute of Mental Health, NIMH.NIH.gov
- OCD San Francisco Bay Area, OCDBayArea.org
- OCD-UK, OCDUK.org (United Kingdom)

REFERENCES

Beck, Judith. *Cognitive Behavior Therapy: Basics and Beyond. 2nd Edition*. New York: The Guilford Press, 2011.

Bell, Jeff. *Rewind, Replay, Repeat: A Memoir of Obsessive-Compulsive Disorder*. Center City, MN: Hazelden, 2007.

Browne, H. A., S. L. Gair, J. M. Scharf, and D. E. Grice. "Genetics of Obsessive-Compulsive Disorder and Related Disorders." *Psychiatric Clinics of North America* 37, no. 3 (2014): 319–35.

Burns, David D. *Feeling Good: The New Mood Therapy*. New York: Avon Books, 1980.

Chansky, Tamar E. *Freeing Your Child from Obsessive-Compulsive Disorder*. New York: Three Rivers Press, 2000.

Clark, David A. and Shelley Rhyno. "Unwanted Intrusive Thoughts in Nonclinical Individuals: Implications for Clinical Disorders." *Intrusive Thoughts in Clinical Disorders: Theory, Research, and Treatment*. New York: The Guilford Press, 2005.

Cromer, K. R., N. B. Schmidt, and D. L. Murphy. "An Investigation of Traumatic Life Events and Obsessive-Compulsive Disorder." *Behaviour Research and Therapy* 45, no. 7 (2007): 1683–91.

Davis, Martha, Elizabeth Robbins Eshelman, and Matthew McKay. *The Relaxation and Stress Reduction Workbook. Sixth Edition*. Oakland, CA: New Harbinger, 2008.

Fabricant, L. E., J. S. Abramowitz, J. P. Dehlin, and M. P. Twohig. "A Comparison of Two Brief Interventions for Obsessional Thoughts: Exposure and Acceptance." *Journal of Cognitive Psychotherapy* 27, no. 3 (2013): 195–209.

Greenberger, Dennis and Christine A. Padesky. *Mind Over Mood, Second Edition: Change How You Feel by Changing the Way You Think*. New York: The Guilford Press, 2015.

Greeson, Jeffrey M. "Mindfulness Research Update: 2008." *Complementary Health Practice Review* 14, no. 1 (2009): 10–18, https://www.ncbi.nlm.nih.gov/pmc/articles/PMC2679512.

Harris, Russ. "Embracing Your Demons: An Overview of Acceptance and Commitment Therapy." *Psychotherapy in Australia* 12, no. 4 (August 2006): 70–76.

Harris, Russ. *The Happiness Trap: How to Stop Struggling and Start Living: A Guide to ACT*. Boston: Trumpeter, 2008.

Hayes, Steven C. and Spencer Smith. *Get Out of Your Mind and Into Your Life: The New Acceptance and Commitment Therapy*. Oakland, CA: New Harbinger, 2005.

Kabat-Zinn, Jon. *Full Catastrophe Living (Revised Edition): Using the Wisdom of Your Body and Mind to Face Stress, Pain, and Illness*. New York: Bantam, 2013.

Kircanski, K., and T. S. Peris. "Exposure and Response Prevention Process Predicts Treatment Outcome in Youth with OCD." *Journal of Abnormal Psychology* 43, no. 3 (April 2015): 543–52.

Linehan, Marsha M. *Skills Training Manual for Treating Borderline Personality Disorder*. New York: The Guilford Press, 1993.

McKay, D., D. Sookman, F. Neziroglu, S. Wilhelm, D. J. Stein, M. Kyrios, K. Matthews, and D. Veale. "Efficacy of Cognitive-Behavioral Therapy for Obsessive-Compulsive Disorder." *Psychiatry Research* 225 (2015): 236–46.

Murphy, Terry Weible, Michael A. Jenike, and Edward E. Zine. *Life in Rewind: The Story of a Young Courageous Man Who Persevered Over OCD and the Harvard Doctor Who Broke All the Rules to Help Him*. New York: William Morrow Paperbacks, 2010.

Nestadt, G., M. Grados, and J. F. Samuels. "Genetics of OCD." *Psychiatric Clinics of North America* 33, no. 1 (2010): 141–58.

Osborn, Ian. *Tormenting Thoughts and Secret Rituals: The Hidden Epidemic of Obsessive-Compulsive Disorder*. New York: Pantheon Books, 1998.

Pinto Wagner, Aureen and Paul A. Jutton. *Up and Down the Worry Hill: A Children's Book about Obsessive-Compulsive Disorder and Its Treatment* (Third Revised Edition), Lighthouse Press, Inc., 2004.

Strauss, C., C. Rosten, M. Hayward, L. Lea, E. Forrester, and A. M. Jones. "Mindfulness-based Exposure and Response Prevention for Obsessive Compulsive Disorder: Study Protocol for a Pilot Randomised Controlled Trial." *Trials* 16 (2015): 167, https://doi.org/10.1186/s13063-015-0664-7.

Targum, S. D. "Identification and Treatment of Antidepressant Tachyphylaxis." *Innovations in Clinical Neuroscience* 11, no. 3–4 (2014): 24–28.

Tolin, David F., Randy O. Frost, and Gail Steketee. *Buried in Treasures: Help for Compulsive Acquiring, Saving, and Hoarding*. Oxford: Oxford University Press. 2007.

Twohig, M. P., J. S. Abramowitz, E. J. Bluett, L. E. Fabricant, R. J. Jacoby, K. L. Morrison, L. Reuman, and B. M. Smith. "Exposure Therapy for OCD from an Acceptance and Commitment Therapy (ACT) Framework." *Journal of Obsessive-Compulsive and Related Disorders* 6 (2015): 167–73.

Twohig, M. P., S. C. Hayes, J. C. Plumb, L. D. Pruitt, A. B. Collins, H. Hazlett-Stevens, and M. R. Woidneck. "A Randomized Clinical Trial of Acceptance and Commitment Therapy versus Progressive Relaxation Training for Obsessive-Compulsive Disorder." *Journal of Consulting and Clinical Psychology* 78, no. 5 (2010): 705–16, https://doi.org/10.1037/a0020508.

Veale, D. "Cognitive-Behavioural Therapy for Obsessive-Compulsive Disorder." *Advances in Psychiatric Treatment* 13 (2007): 438–46, https://doi.org/10.1192/apt.bp.107.003699.

Veale, D., M. Freeston, G. Krebs, I. Heyman, and P. Salkovskis. "Risk Assessment and Management in Obsessive-Compulsive Disorder." *Advances in Psychiatric Treatment* 15 (2009): 332–43, https://doi.org/10.1192/apt.bp.107.004705.

Wegner, D. M., D. J. Schneider, S. R. Carter III, and T. L. White. "Parodoxical Effects of Thought Suppression." *Journal of Personality and Social Psychology* 53, no. 1 (July 1987): 5–13.

Wolpe, Joseph. *The Practice of Behavior Therapy*. Amsterdam: Elsevier Science & Technology Books, 1973.

BLANK WORKSHEETS

Find additional copies of these worksheets online at callistomediabooks.com/OCDworkbook

The Downward Arrow Technique

Automatic thought:

What does that thought mean about me?

And what would that mean about me?

And if true, what would that mean about me?

Core belief:

Automatic thought:

What does that thought mean about me?

And what would that mean about me?

And if true, what would that mean about me?

Core belief:

Automatic thought:

What does that thought mean about me?

And what would that mean about me?

And if true, what would that mean about me?

Core belief:

ERP Worksheets

ERP WORKSHEET #1

DATE/TIME	ERP PRACTICED	SUDS RATING	OBSERVATIONS
		Initial: After 10 mins: After 20 mins: After 30 mins: After 40 mins: After 50 mins: After 60 mins:	

ERP WORKSHEET #2

DATE/TIME	ERP PRACTICED	SUDS RATING	OBSERVATIONS
		Initial: After 10 mins: After 20 mins: After 30 mins: After 40 mins: After 50 mins: After 60 mins:	

ERP WORKSHEET #3

DATE/TIME	ERP PRACTICED	SUDS RATING	OBSERVATIONS
		Initial: After 10 mins: After 20 mins: After 30 mins: After 40 mins: After 50 mins: After 60 mins:	

ERP WORKSHEET #4

DATE/TIME	ERP PRACTICED	SUDS RATING	OBSERVATIONS
		Initial: After 10 mins: After 20 mins: After 30 mins: After 40 mins: After 50 mins: After 60 mins:	

ERP WORKSHEET #5

DATE/TIME	ERP PRACTICED	SUDS RATING	OBSERVATIONS
		Initial: After 10 mins: After 20 mins: After 30 mins: After 40 mins: After 50 mins: After 60 mins:	

ERP WORKSHEET #6

DATE/TIME	ERP PRACTICED	SUDS RATING	OBSERVATIONS
		Initial: After 10 mins: After 20 mins: After 30 mins: After 40 mins: After 50 mins: After 60 mins:	

Thought Records

Date/time: ______________________________

Situation: ______________________________

____

Automatic thought: ______________________________

____

Evidence that the thought is TRUE: ______________________________

____

Evidence that the thought may not be TRUE: ______________________________

____

More rational thought: ______________________________

____

How much do you believe the thought now? ______________________________

Date/time: ______________________________

Situation: ______________________________

____

Automatic thought: ______________________________

____

Evidence that the thought is TRUE: ______________________________

____

Evidence that the thought may not be TRUE: ______________________________

____

More rational thought: ______________________________

____

How much do you believe the thought now? ______________________________

Date/time: ___

Situation: ___

___

Automatic thought: ___

___

Evidence that the thought is TRUE: ___

___

Evidence that the thought may not be TRUE: ___

___

More rational thought: ___

___

How much do you believe the thought now? ___

INDEX

ACKNOWLEDGMENTS

WRITING A BOOK had been a goal of mine for many years, though somehow life kept getting in the way. This past year, however, I had the good fortune of being contacted by Callisto Media about writing a workbook on OCD. I was very excited at the prospect, though as a first-time author I truly had no idea what it would entail. Fortunately, I had plenty of help. I'd first like to thank my editor, Nana K. Twumasi, for her guidance and patience throughout the process. I especially appreciated her sensitivity to the subject matter, and her dedication to producing a quality resource which I believe will be of great benefit to those living with the disorder.

Much of my experience in learning how to treat OCD has come from my long association with the International OCD Foundation. I would like to thank the IOCDF not just for helping me become a better clinician, but for all the organization does to help those living with OCD and related disorders. Similarly, I'd like to thank Mary Weinstein, the president of our local IOCDF affiliate organization, OCD San Francisco Bay Area. Her leadership has been an integral part of what has enabled the organization to offer support to those who live with OCD throughout the region.

I would also like to thank my clients, without whom this book could never have been written. You have let me into your lives, trusted me, and provided me with the greatest gift a therapist could ask for her: your recovery. Your courage in confronting such an unrelenting disorder continues to be an inspiration to me.

Of course, there's my family. I would like to thank my wife, Nancy, for her love and understanding how important this project has been to me, and for putting up with the many late nights and weekends I spent writing. My mother, Dorothy, for always believing in me, and my siblings Craig, Keith, Russell, and especially Suzy for their unconditional support. And lastly, my daughter Allison, who reminds me every day of what it means to feel truly grateful.

ABOUT THE AUTHOR

SCOTT M. GRANET, LCSW, received his master's degree in social work from New York University and has specialized in the treatment of OCD and related disorders for 30 years. In 2008, he opened the OCD-BDD Clinic of Northern California in Redwood City. In addition to his clinical work, Mr. Granet teaches continuing education classes for mental health professionals on OCD, body dysmorphic disorder, and anxiety disorders for various educational institutions throughout the United States. The focus of these classes is to educate clinicians so they can develop the cognitive behavioral therapy (CBT) skills needed to both assess for and treat these underserved disorders. He has also appeared on local and national radio and TV shows, has published various articles, and has presented at conferences worldwide. He was a founding board member for OCD San Francisco, an affiliate organization of the International OCD Foundation, and continues to serve in that capacity.

CPSIA information can be obtained
at www.ICGtesting.com
Printed in the USA
BVHW060508140819
555790BV00006BA/13/P